Penguin Books
French Phrase Book
Henri Orteu and Jillian Norman

French Phrase Book

Henri Orteu and Jillian Norman

Penguin Books Ltd, Harmondsworth,
Middlesex, England
Penguin Books Inc., 7110 Ambassador Road,
Baltimore, Maryland 21207, U.S.A.
Penguin Books Australia Ltd, Ringwood,
Victoria, Australia

First published 1968
Reprinted 1969, 1970, 1971

Made and printed in Great Britain by
Hazell Watson & Viney Ltd, Aylesbury, Bucks
Set in Monotype Plantin

CONTENTS

Introduction 7

Pronunciation guide 9

Essential Grammar 13

First things 24
Essentials 24
Questions and requests 24
Useful statements 25
Language problems 26
Polite phrases 27
Greetings and hospitality 28

Signs and public notices 30
Some useful abbreviations 32

Money 33
Currency tables 33

Travel 35
On arrival 35
Buying a ticket 36
Signs to look for at stations 37
By train and underground 39
By air 41
By ship 42
By bus or coach 43
By taxis 44

Directions 46

Motoring 48
At the garage – repairs, etc. 49
Parts of the car – vocabulary 53
Tyre pressure table 57

Accommodation 58
Booking a room 58
In your room 60
At the reception desk 62
Departure 64

Restaurant 65
Going to a restaurant 65
Ordering 66
Drinks 67
Paying 68
Breakfast 69
Restaurant vocabulary 70

The menu 73

Shopping 86
Where to go 86
In the shop 86
Choosing 87
Complaints 89
Paying 89
Clothes and shoes 90
Clothing sizes 91
Chemist 93
Toilet requisites 94

Photography 94
Food 96
Tobacconist 97
Newspapers, books, writing materials 98
Laundry and cleaning 98
Repairs 99

Barber and Hairdresser 101

Post Office 103
Letters and telegrams 103
Telephoning 104

Sightseeing 107

Entertainment 110

Sports and games 112

On the beach 114

Camping and walking 116

At the doctor's 118

At the dentist's 121

Problems and accidents 123

Time and dates 125

Public holidays 128

Numbers 129

Weights and measures 131

Vocabulary 137

INTRODUCTION

In this series of phrase books only those words and phrases that are essential to the traveller have been included. For easy reference the phrases are divided into several sections, each one dealing with a different situation. Some of the French phrases are marked with an asterisk – these attempt to give an indication of the kind of reply you may get to your questions.

At the end of the book is an extensive vocabulary list and here a pronunciation guide is given for each word. In addition there is an explanation of French pronunciation at the beginning of the book and a brief survey of the essential points of grammar. It would be advisable to read these sections before starting to use the book.

FRENCH PRONUNCIATION

The pronunciation guide is intended for people with no knowledge of French. As far as possible the system is based on English pronunciation. This means that complete accuracy may sometimes be lost for the sake of simplicity, but the reader should be able to understand French pronunciation, and make himself understood, if he reads this section carefully. In addition, each word in the vocabulary is given with a pronunciation guide.

Vowels

French vowels are much purer than English.

a	as 'a' in apple	symbol **a**	famille – fa-mee
ai,e	as 'e' in pen	symbol **e**	mettre – metr vinaigre – vee-negr
é,er	as 'ay' in pay	symbol **ay**	élastique – ay-las-teek marcher – mar-shay
è,er	as 'ai' in pair	symbol **ai**	père – pair travers – tra-vair
eu+l,r	not an English sound, but it is a little like the sound in 'her'	symbol **œ**	beurre – bœr seul – sœl
e,eu	this is like the vowel sound in 'the'	symbol **e^r**	le, je – le^r, zhe^r mercredi – mair-kre^r-dee
i	as 'ee' in meet NB i before e is usually pronounced 'y'	symbol **ee**	merci – mair-see fermier – fair-myay

o	as 'o' in olive	symbol **o**	poste – post pomme – pom
ou	as 'oo' in moon	symbol **oo**	ouvert – oo-vair tout – too
u	not an English sound; round the lips and push them forwards as though to say 'oo' and try to say 'ee'	symbol **u^{e}**	rue – ru^{e} musée – mu^{e}-say
au,o	as 'oh'	symbol **oh**	chaud – shoh eau – oh
oi	as 'wa'	symbol **wa**	voiture – vwa-tu^{e}r
ui	as 'we'	symbol **we**	pluie – plwee oui – we

Nasals

These sounds should be made through the nose, but without pronouncing the 'n'.

an (m) **en (m)**	symbol **ah^{n}**	vent – vah^{n} manger – mah^{n}-zhay
on (m)	symbol **oh^{n}**	on – oh^{n} pont – poh^{n}
ain (m) **in (m)**	symbol **a^{n}**	faim – fa^{n} vin – va^{n} bien – bya^{n}
un (m)	symbol **e^{n}**	brun – bre^{n} un – e^{n}

Consonants

ch	as 'sh' in ship	symbol **sh**	chercher – shair-shay
j,g+e,i	as 's' in pleasure	symbol **zh**	garage – garazh
g+a,o,u	as 'g' in good; in pronunciation guide 'g' is sometimes followed by 'h' to make this clearer		guide – gheed
gn	pronounced as 'n-y'	symbol **n-y**	peigne – pen-y
h	not pronounced – but sometimes aspirate		hôtel – otel
ill,ail, euill	pronounced as 'y'	symbol **y**	fille – fee-y ail – a-y
qu	always pronounced 'k' not 'kw' as in English	symbol **k**	qualité – ka-lee-tay
r	is rolled more than in English		
s	as 's' in sip as 'z' in visit final 's' is not pronounced (unless the next word starts with a consonant or silent 'h')	symbol **s** symbol **z**	sucr – su^{e}kr visite – vee-zeet

The final consonant of a French word is not normally pronounced. However, if the next word begins with a vowel or silent 'h', the final consonant is then pronounced as the first sound of that word, e.g. les

Anglais – lay-zah^{n}-glay. This kind of liaison is indicated in the vocabulary.

French has no stress as in English. It has a musical inflexion which runs throughout a sentence rather than individual words. Syllables have more or less equal value (unlike English), although the last pronounced syllable is sometimes very lightly stressed. Avoid anything resembling strong English stress, but you can give a little weight to the end of French words.

ESSENTIAL GRAMMAR

GENDER OF NOUNS

In French nouns are either masculine or feminine.

e.g. *m*	*f*
le livre (the book)	la table (the table)
le train (the train)	la route (the road)

PLURAL OF NOUNS

To form the plural most nouns add -s. Those ending in -eau, -eu, and some ending in -ou take -x; most ending in -al change to -aux.

sing	*pl*
le coiffeur (the hairdresser)	les coiffeurs (the hairdressers)
le bateau (the boat)	les bateaux (the boats)
l'animal (the animal)	les animaux (the animals)

THE DEFINITE ARTICLE (the)

	m	*f*
sing	le père (the father)	la mère (the mother)
pl	les pères (the fathers)	les mères (the mothers)

Before a singular noun beginning with a vowel or a silent 'h' le (*m*), la (*f*) become l'

l'hôtel (the hotel)	l'auto (the car)
l'homme (the man)	l'adresse (the address)

THE INDEFINITE ARTICLE (a, an)

	m	*f*
sing	un hôtel (a hotel)	une auto (a car)

THE PARTITIVE ARTICLE (some, any)

	m	*f*
sing	du (= de + le) beurre (some butter)	de la confiture (some jam)
pl	des (= de + les) biscuits (some biscuits)	des pommes (some apples)

ADJECTIVES

Adjectives agree with the nouns they describe in gender and number. To form the feminine most adjectives add -e to the masculine. To form the plural most adjectives add -s.

	m	*f*
sing	un camion vert (a green lorry)	une auto verte (a green car)
pl	des camions verts (green lorries)	des autos vertes (green cars)

Adjectives are usually placed after the noun, but there are some exceptions.

POSSESSIVE ADJECTIVES

These adjectives agree in gender and number with the object possessed.

	m	*f*	*pl*
my	mon passeport	ma valise	mes enfants
his, her, its	son ,,	sa ,,	ses ,,
our	notre ,,	notre ,,	nos ,,
your	votre ,,	votre ,,	vos ,,
their	leur ,,	leur ,,	leurs ,,

DEMONSTRATIVE ADJECTIVES (this, these, that, those)

	m		*f*	
sing	ce monsieur	this/that gentleman	cette dame	this/that lady
pl	ces hommes	these/those men	ces femmes	these/those women

Before a masculine singular noun beginning with a vowel or a silent 'h' cet is used instead of ce.
e.g. cet homme this/that man cet arbre this/that tree

RELATIVE PRONOUNS (who, whom, which, that)

subject	qui	La rue qui mène à la gare	the street that leads to the station
object	que	L'hôtelier que je connais	the hotel keeper whom I know

PERSONAL PRONOUNS

subject		*direct object*		*indirect object of a verb*		*preceded by a preposition*
I	je	me	me	to me	me	moi
you	tu	you	te	to you	te	toi
he, it	il	him, it	le	to him, her, it	lui	lui
she, it	elle	her, it	la	to her, it	lui	elle
we	nous	us	nous	to us	nous	nous
you	vous	you	vous	to you	vous	vous
they *m*	ils	them *m, f*	les	to them *m*	leur	eux
they *f*	elles			to them *f*	leur	elles

Object pronouns are usually placed between the subject and the verb.

e.g. Je le vois	I see him	Je l'aide	I help him, her, it
Il me parle	he speaks to me	Nous les mangeons	we eat them

VERBS

Verb forms are too difficult to discuss in detail here, but we give present, future, and perfect tenses of the regular verb patterns, and some of the more common irregular verbs. The perfect tense is made up of the present tense of *avoir*, or sometimes *être*, with the past participle of the verb.

The second person singular *tu* is only used when speaking to children, close friends or relatives, and animals. In all other cases use *vous*.

Être – *to be*

Present		*Future*		*Past*	
je suis	*I am*	je serai	*I shall be, etc.*	j'ai été	*I was/have been, etc.*
tu es	*you are*	tu seras		tu as été	
il/elle est	*he/she is*	il sera		il a été	
nous sommes	*we are*	nous serons		nous avons été	
vous êtes	*you are*	vous serez		vous avez été	
ils/elles sont	*they are*	ils seront		ils ont été	

Avoir – *to have*

Present		Future		Past	
j'ai	*I have*	j'aurai	*I shall have, etc.*	j'ai eu	*I had/have had, etc.*
tu as	*you have*	tu auras		tu as eu	
il/elle a	*he/she has*	il aura		il a eu	
nous avons	*we have*	nous aurons		nous avons eu	
vous avez	*you have*	vous aurez		vous avez eu	
ils/elles ont	*they have*	ils auront		ils ont eu	

REGULAR VERBS

Aimer – *to like*; verbs ending in **-er**

Present	Future	Past
j'aim**e**	j'aimer**ai**	j'ai aim**é**, etc.
tu aim**es**	tu aimer**as**	
il aim**e**	il aimer**a**	
nous aim**ons**	nous aimer**ons**	
vous aim**ez**	vous aimer**ez**	
ils aim**ent**	ils aimer**ont**	

Finir – *to finish*; verbs ending in **-ir**

Present	Future	Past
je fin**is**	je finir**ai**	j'ai fin**i**, etc.
tu fin**is**	tu finir**as**	
il fin**it**	il finir**a**	
nous fin**issons**	nous finir**ons**	
vous fin**issez**	vous finir**ez**	
ils fin**issent**	ils finir**ont**	

Vendre – *to sell*; verbs ending in **-re**

Present	*Future*	*Past*
je vend**s**	je vendr**ai**	j'ai vend**u**, etc.
tu vend**s**	tu vendr**as**	
il vend	il vendr**a**	
nous vend**ons**	nous vendr**ons**	
vous vend**ez**	vous vendr**ez**	
ils vend**ent**	ils vendr**ont**	

IRREGULAR VERBS

Aller – *to go*

Present	*Future*	*Past*
je vais	j'irai	je suis allé
tu vas	tu iras	tu es allé
il va	il ira	il est allé
nous allons	nous irons	nous sommes allés
vous allez	vous irez	vous êtes allés
ils vont	ils iront	ils sont allés

Boire – *to drink*

Present	*Future*	*Past*
je bois	je boirai	j'ai bu, etc.
tu bois	tu boiras	
il boit	il boira	
nous buvons	nous boirons	
vous buvez	vous boirez	
ils boivent	ils boiront	

Connaître – *to know (someone)*

Present	*Future*	*Past*
je connais	je connaîtrai	j'ai connu, etc.
tu connais	tu connaîtras	
il connaît	il connaîtra	
nous connaissons	nous connaîtrons	
vous connaissez	vous connaîtrez	
ils connaissent	ils connaîtront	

Devoir – *to have to, must*

Present	*Future*	*Past*
je dois	je devrai	j'ai dû, etc.
tu dois	tu devras	
il doit	il devra	
nous devons	nous devrons	
vous devez	vous devrez	
ils doivent	ils devront	

Dire – *to say*

Present	*Future*	*Past*
je dis	je dirai	j'ai dit, etc.
tu dis	tu diras	
il dit	il dira	
nous disons	nous dirons	
vous dites	vous direz	
ils disent	ils diront	

Faire – *to make, do*

Present	*Future*	*Past*
je fais	je ferai	j'ai fait, etc.
tu fais	tu feras	
il fait	il fera	
nous faisons	nous ferons	
vous faites	vous ferez	
ils font	ils feront	

Lire – *to read*

Present	*Future*	*Past*
je lis	je lirai	j'ai lu, etc.
tu lis	tu liras	
il lit	il lira	
nous lisons	nous lirons	
vous lisez	vous lirez	
ils lisent	ils liront	

Mettre – *to put*

Present	*Future*	*Past*
je mets	je mettrai	j'ai mis, etc.
tu mets	tu mettras	
il met	il mettra	
nous mettons	nous mettrons	
vous mettez	vous mettrez	
ils mettent	ils mettront	

Partir – *to leave*

Present	*Future*	*Past*
je pars	je partirai	je suis parti, etc.
tu pars	tu partiras	
il part	il partira	
nous partons	nous partirons	
vous partez	vous partirez	
ils partent	ils partiront	

Pouvoir – *to be able, can*

Present	*Future*	*Past*
je peux	je pourrai	j'ai pu, etc.
tu peux	tu pourras	
il peut	il pourra	
nous pouvons	nous pourrons	
vous pouvez	vous pourrez	
ils peuvent	ils pourront	

Prendre – *to take*

Present	*Future*	*Past*
je prends	je prendrai	j'ai pris, etc.
tu prends	tu prendras	
il prend	il prendra	
nous prenons	nous prendrons	
vous prenez	vous prendrez	
ils prennent	ils prendront	

Savoir – *to know (something)*

Present	*Future*	*Past*
je sais	je saurai	j'ai su, etc.
tu sais	tu sauras	
il sait	il saura	
nous savons	nous saurons	
vous savez	vous saurez	
ils savent	ils sauront	

Venir – *to come*

Present	*Future*	*Past*
je viens	je viendrai	je suis venu, etc.
tu viens	tu viendras	
il vient	il viendra	
nous venons	nous viendrons	
vous venez	vous viendrez	
ils viennent	ils viendront	

Voir – *to see*

Present	*Future*	*Past*
je vois	je verrai	j'ai vu, etc.
tu vois	tu verras	
il voit	il verra	
nous voyons	nous verrons	
vous voyez	vous verrez	
ils voient	ils verront	

Vouloir – *to want*

Present	*Future*	*Past*
je veux	je voudrai	j'ai voulu, etc.
tu veux	tu voudras	
il veut	il voudra	
nous voulons	nous voudrons	
vous voulez	vous voudrez	
ils veulent	ils voudront	

Negative

The negative is formed by putting ne before the verb and pas after. Ne becomes n' before a vowel.

e.g.			
Je ne suis pas français	I am not French	Je n'ai pas d'argent	I've no money

FIRST THINGS

Essentials

Yes	Oui
No	Non
Please	S'il vous plaît
Thank you	Merci
Yes, please	Oui, merci
No, thank you[1]	(Non) merci

Questions and requests

Where is/are . . . ?	Où est/sont . . . ?
When ?	Quand ?
How much is/are . . . ?	Combien coûte/coûtent . . . ?
How far ?	C'est à quelle distance ?
What's that ?	Qu'est-ce que c'est ?

1. In reply to an offer of any kind *merci* means 'no thank you'. To accept, one should say *oui, merci* or *oui, s'il vous plaît.*

What do you want?	Que voulez-vous?
What must I do?	Que dois-je faire?
Have you . . .?	Avez-vous . . .?
Is there . . .?	Y a-t-il . . .?
Have you seen . . .?	Avez-vous vu . . .?
May I have . . .?	Pourrais-je avoir . . .?
I want/should like . . .	Je veux/voudrais . . .
I don't want . . .	Je ne veux pas . . .

Useful statements

Here is/are . . .	Voici . . .
I like it	J'aime ça
I don't like it	Je n'aime pas ça
I know	Je sais
I don't know	Je ne sais pas
I didn't know	Je ne savais pas
I think so	Je crois que oui
I'm hungry	J'ai faim
I'm thirsty	J'ai soif

I'm tired	Je suis fatigué
I'm in a hurry	Je suis pressé
I'm ready	Je suis prêt
Leave me alone	Laissez-moi tranquille
Just a moment	* Une minute/un instant
This way, please	* Par ici, s'il vous plaît
Take a seat	* Asseyez-vous
Come in!	* Entrez!
It's cheap	C'est bon marché
It's too expensive	C'est trop cher
That's all	C'est tout
You're right	Vous avez raison
You're wrong	Vous avez tort

Language problems

I'm English/American	Je suis anglais(-e)/américain(-e)
Do you speak English?	Parlez-vous anglais?
I don't speak French	Je ne parle pas français
I don't understand	Je ne comprends pas

Would you say that again, please?	Voulez-vous répéter, s'il vous plaît?
Please speak slowly	Parlez lentement, je vous prie

Polite phrases

Sorry	Pardon
Excuse me	Excusez-moi
That's all right (*in reply to* excuse me)	Il n'y a pas de mal
Not at all/don't mention it (*after thanks*)	Il n'y a pas de quoi/je vous en prie
Don't worry	Ne vous inquiétez pas
It doesn't matter	Cela ne fait rien/cela n'a pas d'importance
I beg your pardon? What?	Comment?
Am I disturbing you?	Est-ce que je vous dérange?
I'm sorry to have troubled you	Je suis désolé de vous avoir dérangé
Good/that's fine	Bien/c'est parfait

Greetings and hospitality

Good morning/good day/ good afternoon[1]	*when meeting* Bonjour monsieur/ madame/mademoiselle *when departing* Au revoir
Good evening	Bonsoir
Good night	*only when going to bed* Bonne nuit/*otherwise* Bonsoir
How are you?	Comment allez-vous?
Very well, thank you	Très bien, merci
Good-bye	Au revoir
See you soon	À bientôt
See you tomorrow	À demain
Have you met my wife?	Vous connaissez ma femme?
May I introduce you to my husband?	Puis-je vous présenter mon mari?
Glad to know you	Heureux de faire votre connaissance
What's your name?	Comment vous appelez-vous?
What's your address?	Quelle est votre adresse?
What's your telephone number?	Quel est votre numéro de téléphone?

1. *Bonjour, bonsoir, au revoir* should be followed by either *monsieur, madame, mademoiselle* (sing.) or *messieurs, mesdames, mesdemoiselles* (pl.) or *messieurs dames* (when greeting a group of people of both sexes).

Where are you staying?	Où logez-vous?
Where are you from?	D'où êtes-vous?
What are you doing this evening?	Que faites-vous ce soir?
Would you like to have dinner/coffee with me?	Voulez-vous dîner/prendre le café avec moi?
Would you like to go to the museum/for a walk/dancing?	Voulez-vous aller au musée/faire une promenade/danser?
Would you like a drink?	* Voulez-vous boire quelque chose?
Would you like a cigarette?	* Voulez-vous une cigarette?
Can I offer you anything?	* Puis-je vous offrir quelque chose?
Help yourself	* Servez-vous
Thanks for having me	Merci de votre hospitalité
Thanks for the invitation	Merci de votre invitation
Bon voyage	Bon voyage
Good luck/all the best	Bonne chance

SIGNS AND PUBLIC NOTICES[1]

Ascenseur	Lift/elevator
Attention	Caution
Banque	Bank
Caisse	Cashier's desk
Chambre à louer	Room to let
Chambres libres	Vacancies
Commissariat de police[2]	Police station
Complet	Full/no vacancies/no seats
Dames	Ladies
Danger	Danger
Défense d'entrer	Private/no entry
Défense d'entrer sous peine d'amende	Trespassers will be prosecuted
Défense de fumer	No smoking
Eau non potable	(Water) not for drinking
Eau potable	Drinking water
Entrée	Entrance
Entrée interdite	No admission
Entrée libre	Admission free
Entrez sans frapper	Please enter
Fermé	Closed
Frappez	Knock

1. See also MOTORING (p. 48)

2. See note, p. 123

Gendarmerie[1]	Police station
Guide	Guide
Interprète	Interpreter
Issue de secours	Emergency exit
Libre	Vacant/free/unoccupied
Messieurs	Gentlemen
Ne pas toucher	Do not touch
Occupé	Engaged/occupied
Ouvert	Open
P. et T.	Post office
Passage interdit	No admission
Piétons	Pedestrians
Places debout seulement	Standing room only
Prière de ne pas . . .	You are requested not to . . .
Privé	Private
Renseignements	Information
Réservé	Reserved
Sonnez	Ring
Sortie	Exit
Sortie de secours	Emergency exit
Tenez votre droite	Keep right
Toilettes	Lavatory/toilets

1. See note, p. 123.

Some useful abbreviations

P. et T. (Postes et Télécommunications), formerly P.T.T.	Post Office
R.F. (République Française)	French Republic
O.R.T.F. (Radiodiffusion-télévision française)	TV and broadcasting service
S.N.C.F. (Société nationale des chemins de fer français)	French railways

MONEY[1]

Is there an exchange bureau near here?	Y a-t-il un bureau de change près d'ici?
Do you cash traveller's cheques?	Acceptez-vous les chèques de voyage?
Where can I cash traveller's cheques?	Où puis-je encaisser des chèques de voyage?
I want to change some English/American money	Je voudrais changer des livres sterling/des dollars
How much do I get for a pound/dollar?	Combien vaut la livre/le dollar?
Can you give me some small change?	Pourriez-vous me donner de la monnaie?
Sign here, please	* Signez ici s'il vous plaît
Go to the cashier	* Allez à la caisse

FRANCE[2] (1 Franc = 100 Centimes)

1 F	= 7½p or 1/6d	1 F	= 18 cents
10 F	= 75p or 15/-	10 F	= $1.80
50 F	= £3.75 or £3/15/-	50 F	= $9.00
100 F	= £7.50 or £7/10/-	100 F	= $18.00
£1	= 13.33F	$1	= 5.55F

1. In France banks are open from 9 a.m. to 12 noon, and from 2 to 4 p.m. They are closed on Saturdays and Sundays. In Switzerland they are open from 8 or 8.30 a.m. to 5 p.m., closed Saturday and Sunday. In Belgium they open from 10 a.m. to 12 noon, and from 2 to 4 p.m., closed Saturday and Sunday.

2. Note that in France old franc coinage is still in circulation alongside the new. Old franc notes have been overstamped with their new value (100 times less – e.g. 1000 old francs = 10F). The former 100 franc coin is now worth 1F, and the former 1 franc coin 1 centime.

SWITZERLAND (1 Franc = 100 Centimes)

1 Sw. Fr.	= 9½p or 1/11d	1 Sw. Fr.	= 23 cents
10 Sw. Fr.	= 95p or 19/1d	10 Sw. Fr.	= $2.29
50 Sw. Fr.	= £4.76 or £4/15/3d	50 Sw. Fr.	= $11.43
100 Sw. Fr.	= £9.52 or £9/10/6d	100 Sw. Fr.	= $22.86
£1	= 10.50 Sw. Fr.	$1	= 4.375 Sw. Fr.

BELGIUM (1 Franc = 100 Centimes)

1 F	= 1p or 2d	1 F	= 2 cents
10 F	= 8p or 1/7d	10 F	= 19 cents
50 F	= 39p or 7/10d	50 F	= 94 cents
100 F	= 79p or 15/9d	100 F	= $1.89
£1	= 127 F	$1	= 53 F

These rates of exchange are approximate only and subject to variations.

TRAVEL

On arrival

Customs	* Douane
Passport control	* Contrôle des passeports
Your passport, please	* Votre passeport, s'il vous plaît
Are you together?	* Vous êtes ensemble?
I'm travelling alone	Je voyage seul
I'm travelling with my wife/ a friend	Je voyage avec ma femme/ un(e) ami(e)
I'm here on business	Je suis ici pour affaires
on holiday	Je viens passer mes vacances
May I see your green card, please?	Pouvez-vous me montrer votre carte verte?
What is your address in Paris/ France?	* Quelle est votre adresse à Paris/en France?
How long are you staying here?	* Combien de temps pensez-vous rester?
How much money have you got?	* Combien d'argent avez-vous?
I have . . . francs/pounds/ dollars	J'ai . . . francs/livres/dollars
Which is your luggage?	* Quels sont vos bagages?
Have you anything to declare?	* Avez-vous quelque chose à déclarer?
This is my luggage	Voici mes bagages

I have only my personal things in it	Ils ne contiennent que mes affaires personnelles
Open your bag, please	* Ouvrez votre sac, s'il vous plaît
Can I shut my case now?	Puis-je refermer ma valise maintenant?
May I go through?	Puis-je passer?
Where is the information bureau?	Où se trouve le bureau de renseignements?
Porter, here is my luggage	Porteur, voici mes bagages
What is the price for each piece of luggage?	C'est combien par colis?
I shall take this myself	Je porterai cela moi-même
That's not mine	Ce n'est pas à moi
Would you call a taxi?	Pourriez-vous appeler un taxi?
How much do I owe you?	Combien est-ce que je vous dois?

Buying a ticket

Where's the nearest travel agency?	Où se trouve l'agence de voyage la plus proche?
Have you a timetable, please?[1]	Avez-vous un horaire, s'il vous plaît?

1. The equivalent of the British 'ABC Rail Guide' is called 'Indicateur Chaix'.

What's the tourist return fare to . . . ?	Combien coûte le billet touristique pour . . . aller et retour ?
How much is it first class to . . . ?	Combien coûte un billet de première pour . . . ?
A second class single to . . .	Un aller simple en deuxième classe pour . . .
Three singles to . . .	Trois aller simples pour . . .
A return to . . .	Un aller et retour pour . . .
Are there reduced rate tickets ?	Y a-t-il des billets à tarif réduit ?
How long is this ticket valid ?	Combien de temps ce billet est-il valable ?
A book of tickets, please[2]	Un carnet de tickets, s'il vous plaît
Is there a supplementary charge ?	Y a-t-il un supplément à payer ?

Signs to look for at stations, termini, etc.

Arrivals	Arrivée
Booking Office	Location
Buses	Autobus

2. This is only available for bus or tube journeys. It is much cheaper to buy a *carnet* than single tickets for each journey.

Connexions	Correspondances
Departures	Départ
Exchange	Change
Gentlemen	Messieurs
Inquiries	Renseignements
Ladies' Room	Dames
Left Luggage { in / out	Consigne { dépôts / retraits
Lost Property	Bureau des objets trouvés
Main Lines	Grandes lignes
Non-Smoker	Non-Fumeur
Refreshments	Buvette/Buffet
Reservations	Réservations
Smoker	Fumeur
Suburban Lines	Lignes de banlieue
Taxis	Taxis
Tickets	Billets
Underground	Métro (Métropolitain)
Waiting Room	Salle d'attente

By train and underground[1]

RESERVATIONS AND INQUIRIES

Where's the railway station/ tube station?	Où est la gare/la station de métro?
Two seats on the 11.00 tomorrow to . . .	Deux places pour . . . dans le train d'onze heures demain
I want to reserve a sleeper	Je voudrais réserver un wagon-lit
How much does a couchette cost?	Combien coûte une couchette?
I want to register this luggage through to . . .	Je voudrais faire enregistrer ces bagages à destination de . . .
Is it an express or a local train?[2]	Est-ce un train express ou un omnibus?
Is there an earlier/later train?	Y a-t-il un train plus tôt/plus tard?
Is there a restaurant car on the train?	Ce train a-t-il un wagon-restaurant?

1. For help in understanding the answers to these and similar questions see TIME (p. 125), NUMBERS (p. 129), DIRECTIONS (p. 46).

2. Most de-luxe trains in France have a special name according to their destination – e.g. *Flèche d'or* (Paris to London); *Mistral* (Paris to Nice). They are usually first class only.

CHANGING

Is there a through train to . . . ?	Y a-t-il un train direct pour . . . ?
Do I have to change ?	Dois-je changer de train ?
Where do I change ?	Où dois-je changer ?
When is there a connexion to . . . ?	Quand y a-t-il une correspondance pour . . . ?

DEPARTURE

When does the train leave ?	A quelle heure part le train ?
Which platform does the train to . . . leave from ?	Sur quelle voie part le train pour . . . ?
Is this the train for . . . ?	Est-ce bien le train pour . . . ?

ARRIVAL

When does it get to . . . ?	A quelle heure arrive-t-il à . . . ?
Does the train stop at . . . ?	Est-ce que le train s'arrête à . . . ?
How long do we stop here ?	Combien dure l'arrêt ici ?
Is the train late ?	Est-ce que le train a du retard ?
When does the train from . . . get in ?	A quelle heure arrive le train de . . . ?
At which platform ?	Sur quelle voie ?

ON THE TRAIN

We have reserved seats	Nous avons des places réservées
Is this seat free?	Est-ce que cette place est libre?
This seat is taken	Cette place est occupée

By air

Where's the airline office?	Où se trouve l'agence de la compagnie aérienne?
I'd like to book two seats on Monday's plane to . . .	Je voudrais réserver deux places dans l'avion de lundi à destination de . . .
Is there a flight to London on Thursday?	Est-ce qu'il y a un vol à destination de Londres jeudi?
When does it leave/arrive?	A quelle heure est le départ/l'arrivée?
When's the next plane?	Quand part le prochain avion?
Is there a coach from the town to the airport?	Y a-t-il un service d'autocars entre la ville et l'aéroport?
When must I check in?	A quelle heure dois-je me présenter?
Please cancel my reservation to . . .	Annulez ma réservation pour . . . , s'il vous plaît

I'd like to change my reservation	Je voudrais changer ma réservation

By ship

Is there a boat from here to . . . ?	Y a-t-il un bateau pour . . . ?
How long does the boat take ?	Combien dure la traversée ?
How often do the boats leave ?	Tous les combien partent les bateaux ?
Where does the boat put in ?	Où est-ce que le bateau fait escale ?
Does the boat call at . . . ?	Est-ce que le bateau fait escale à . . . ?
When does the next boat leave ?	Quand part le prochain bateau ?
Can I book a single berth cabin ?	Puis-je réserver une cabine à une place ?
How many berths are there in the cabin ?	Combien de places y a-t-il dans la cabine ?
When must we go on board ?	A quelle heure devons-nous embarquer ?
When do we dock ?	A quelle heure accostons-nous ?
How long do we stay in port ?	Combien dure l'escale ?

By bus or coach

Where's the bus station/coach station ?	Où est la station d'autobus/ la gare routière ?
Bus stop	* Arrêt d'autobus
Compulsory stop	* Arrêt fixe
Request stop	* Arrêt facultatif
When does the coach leave ?	A quelle heure part l'autocar ?
When does the coach get to . . . ?	A quelle heure est-ce que l'autocar arrive à . . . ?
What stops does it make ?	Où est-ce qu'il s'arrête ?
How long is the journey ?	Combien dure le voyage/le trajet ?
We want to take a coach tour round the sights	Nous voulons faire une visite touristique en autocar
Is there an excursion to . . . tomorrow ?	Est-ce qu'il y a une excursion à . . . demain ?
When's the next bus ?	A quelle heure est le prochain autobus ?
How often do the buses run ?	Quelle est la fréquence des autobus ?
Has the last bus gone ?	Est-ce que le dernier autobus est parti ?
Does this bus go to the town centre/beach/station ?	Est-ce que cet autobus va au centre de la ville/à la plage/ à la gare ?

Do you go near . . . ?	Allez-vous du côté de . . . ?
Where can I get a bus to . . . ?	Où puis-je prendre un autobus pour . . . ?
Which bus goes to . . . ?	Quel autobus va à (au) . . . ?
I want to go to . . .	Je voudrais aller à (au) . . .
Where do I get off?	Où dois-je descendre ?
The bus to . . . stops over there	* L'autobus pour . . . s'arrête là-bas
A number 30 goes to . . .	* Le trente va à (au) . . .
You must take a number 24	* Il faut prendre le vingt-quatre
(You) get off at the next stop	* (Vous) descendez au prochain arrêt
The buses run every ten minutes/every hour	* L'autobus passe toutes les dix minutes/ toutes les heures

By taxi

Are you free ?	Êtes-vous libre ?
Please take me to the St Sulpice hotel/the station/this address	Conduisez-moi à l'hôtel Saint Sulpice/à la gare/à cette adresse, s'il vous plaît
Can you hurry, I'm late ?	Pouvez-vous aller vite, je suis en retard

I want to see the sights/ shopping centre	Je voudrais voir les curiosités/ les magasins
Please wait for me	Attendez-moi, s'il vous plaît
Stop here	Arrêtez-vous ici
Is it far?	C'est loin?
How much do you charge by the hour/for the day?	Combien coûte l'heure de location/la journée de location?
How much will you charge to take me to . . .?	Quel est le prix de la course pour aller à . . .?
How much is it?	Combien vous dois-je?
That's too much	C'est trop cher

DIRECTIONS

Where is . . . ?	Où est . . . ?
How do I get to . . . ?	Comment fait-on pour aller à . . . ?
How far is it to . . . ?	A quelle distance se trouve . . . ?
How many kilometres ?	Combien de kilomètres ?
How do we get on to the motorway to . . . ?	Comment parvient-on à l'autoroute qui va à . . . ?
Which is the best road to . . . ?	Quelle est la meilleure route pour aller à . . . ?
Is it a good road ?	Est-ce que la route est bonne ?
Is it a motorway ?	Est-ce que c'est une autoroute ?
Is there any danger of avalanches/snowdrifts ?	Risque-t-il d'y avoir des avalanches/des congères ?
Will we get to . . . by evening ?	Pourrons-nous arriver à . . . dans la soirée ?
Where are we now ?	Où sommes-nous maintenant ?
Please show me on the map	Montrez-moi où nous sommes sur la carte, s'il vous plaît
It's that way	* C'est de ce côté
It isn't far	* Ce n'est pas loin
Follow this road for 5 kilometres	* Suivez cette route sur cinq kilomètres
Keep straight on	* Allez tout droit
Turn right at the crossroads	* Tournez à droite au croisement

Take the second road on the left	* Prenez la deuxième route à gauche
Turn right at the traffic-lights	* Tournez à droite aux feux
Turn left after the bridge	* Tournez à gauche après le pont
The best road is the N.7[1]	* La meilleure route est la N.7
Take the D.21 to . . . and ask again	* Prenez la D.21 jusqu'à . . . et demandez à quelqu'un

1. N.7 = *route nationale* 7. All trunk roads are indicated by N followed by a number. D.21 = *route départementale* 21. Secondary roads are indicated by D followed by a number. Motorways are indicated by A followed by a number. A1 = *autoroute* 1 (Paris – Lille).

MOTORING

Where can I hire a car?	Où pourrais-je louer une voiture?
I want to hire a car and a driver/a self drive car	Je voudrais louer une voiture avec chauffeur/une voiture sans chauffeur
How much is it to hire it by the hour/day/week?	Combien coûte la location/ à l'heure/à la journée/à la semaine?
Have you a road map, please?	Avez-vous une carte routière, s'il vous plaît?
Where is a car park?	Où est le parking/le parc de stationnement?
Can I park here?	Peut-on stationner ici?
How long can I park here?	Combien de temps peut-on stationner ici?
May I see your licence, please	* Montrez-moi votre permis de conduire, s'il vous plaît
No parking	* Stationnement interdit
Parking allowed	* Stationnement autorisé
Keep right	* Tenez votre droite
Keep in the right hand lane	* Serrez à droite
Road works ahead	* Attention travaux
Beware of flying stones	* Gravillons
Overtaking prohibited	* Défense de doubler
Road blocked	* Rue barrée
No entry	* Sens interdit

Diversion	* Déviation
One way street	* Sens unique
Speed limit 50 k.p.h.	* Vitesse limite 50 km.h.
Steep hill	* Descente dangereuse
Narrow road	* Route étroite
Winding road	* Route sinueuse/virages
Give way to traffic from the right[1]	* Priorité à droite
Priority over traffic from the right	* Passage protégé
Through traffic	* Toutes directions
Traffic lights	* Feux

At the garage

Where is the nearest petrol station?	Où est le poste d'essence le plus proche?
How far is the next petrol station?	A quelle distance se trouve le prochain poste d'essence?
30 litres of petrol, and please check the oil and water	Trente litres d'essence et vérifiez l'huile et l'eau, s'il vous plaît
10 francs worth of super, please	Dix francs de super, s'il vous plaît

1. It is important to note that, unless there are road signs to the contrary, vehicles coming from the right have priority at road junctions.

Fill her up, please	Faites le plein, s'il vous plaît
How much is petrol a litre?	Combien vaut le litre d'essence?
The oil needs changing	Il faut faire la vidange d'huile
Check the tyre pressures, please[1]	Vérifiez la pression des pneus, s'il vous plaît
Please change the tyre	Changez le pneu, s'il vous plaît
This tyre is flat/punctured	Ce pneu est à plat/crevé
The valve is leaking	La valve perd
The radiator is leaking	Le radiateur perd
Please wash the car	Pouvez-vous laver la voiture, s'il vous plaît?
Can I garage the car here?	Est-ce que je peux garer la voiture ici?
What time does the garage close?	A quelle heure ferme le garage?

Repairs

Have you a breakdown service?	Avez-vous un service de dépannage?
Is there a mechanic?	Y a-t-il un mécanicien?
Where is there an Austin agent?	Où y a-t-il un représentant Austin/une agence Austin?

1. See p. 56

My car's broken down, can you send someone to tow it?	Ma voiture est en panne, pouvez-vous envoyer quelqu'un pour la remorquer?
I want the car serviced	Veuillez faire les vidanges et un graissage complet, s'il vous plaît
The battery is flat, it needs charging	Ma batterie est déchargée, il faut la recharger
My car won't start	Ma voiture ne démarre pas
It's not running properly	Elle ne marche pas bien
The engine is overheating	Le moteur chauffe
The engine is firing badly/ knocks	Le moteur tourne mal/ cogne
It's smoking	Il fume
Can you change this faulty plug?	Pouvez-vous remplacer cette bougie défectueuse?
There's a petrol/oil leak	Il y a une fuite d'essence/ d'huile
There's a smell of petrol/ rubber	Il y a une odeur d'essence/de caoutchouc brûlé
There's a rattle/squeak	Il y a un bruit/quelque chose qui grince
Something is wrong with my car/the engine/the lights/ the clutch/the gearbox/the brakes/the steering	Ma voiture/le moteur/ l'éclairage/l'embrayage/ la boîte de vitesses/les freins/ la direction ne marche(nt) pas bien

I've got electrical/mechanical trouble	J'ai des ennuis électriques/ mécaniques
The carburettor needs adjusting	Le carburateur a besoin d'un réglage
Can you repair it?	Pouvez-vous réparer cela?
How long will it take to repair?	Combien de temps prendra la réparation?
What will it cost?	Combien est-ce que cela coûtera?
When can I pick the car up?	Quand puis-je venir chercher ma voiture?
I need it as soon as possible/ in three hours/in the morning	Je la voudrais le plus tôt possible/dans trois heures/ demain matin
It will take two days	* Cela prendra deux jours
We can repair it temporarily	* Nous pouvons faire une réparation provisoire
We haven't the right spares	* Nous n'avons pas les pièces nécessaires
We have to send for the spares	* Nous devons faire venir les pièces
You will need a new ...	* Il vous faudra un nouveau (une nouvelle) ...
I've lost my car key	J'ai perdu ma clé de contact
The lock is broken/jammed	La serrure est cassée/bloquée

Parts of a car and other vocabulary useful in a garage

accelerate	accélérer
accelerator	l'accélérateur *m*
antifreeze	l'antigel *m*
axle	l'essieu *m*
battery	la batterie
bonnet	le capot
boot/trunk	le coffre
brake	le frein
breakdown	la panne
bumper	le pare-choc
carburettor	le carburateur
choke	le starter
clutch	l'embrayage *m*
crankshaft	le vilebrequin
cylinder	le cylindre
differential gear	le différentiel
dip stick	la jauge d'huile
distributor	le distributeur/l'allumeur *m*
door	la portière

door handle	la poignée
drive (to)	conduire
driver	le chauffeur
dynamo	la dynamo
engine	le moteur
exhaust	l'échappement *m*
fan	le ventilateur
fanbelt	la courroie de ventilateur
flat tyre	le pneu à plat
foglamp	le phare antibrouillard
fuse-box	la boîte à fusibles
gasket	le joint
gear-box	la boîte de vitesses
gear-lever	le lévier du changement de vitesse
gears	les vitesses *m*
grease (to)	graisser
handbrake	le frein à main
heater	le chauffage
horn	le klaxon/l'avertisseur
ignition	l'allumage *m*
ignition key	la clé de contact
indicator (flashing)	le clignotant

jack	le cric
lights – head/side/rear	les phares *m*/les feux de position *m*/les feux rouges *m*
lock/catch	la serrure
mirror	le rétroviseur
number plate	la plaque de police/la plaque d'immatriculation
nut	le boulon
oil	l'huile *f*
petrol	l'essence *f*
petrol can	le bidon d'essence
piston	le piston
points	les vis platinées *f*
propeller shaft	l'arbre de transmission *m*
pump	la pompe
puncture	le crevaison
radiator	le radiateur
rear axle	le pont arrière
reverse (to)	faire marche arrière
reverse	la marche arrière
seat	le siège
shock absorber	l'amortisseur *m*
silencer	le silencieux
spares	les pièces de rechange *f*

spare tyre	le pneu de secours
sparking plug	la bougie
speed	la vitesse
speedometer	le compteur de vitesse
spring	le ressort
stall (to)	caler
starter	le démarreur
steering	la direction
steering wheel	le volant
tank	le réservoir
tappets	les culbuteurs *m*
transmission	la transmission
tyre	le pneu
tyre pressure	la pression des pneus
valve	la soupape
wheel	la roue
window	la vitre/la glace
windscreen	la pare-brise
windscreen washers	le lave-glace
windscreen wipers	l'essuie-glace *m*

Tyre pressure

lb. per sq. in.	kg. per sq. cm.	lb. per sq. in.	kg. per sq. cm.
16	1·1	36	2·5
18	1·3	39	2·7
20	1·4	40	2·8
22	1·5	43	3·0
25	1·7	45	3·2
29	2·0	46	3·2
32	2·3	50	3·5
35	2·5	60	4·2

A rough way to convert lb. per sq. in. to kg. per sq. cm.: multiply by 7 and divide by 100.

ACCOMMODATION[1]

Booking a room

Rooms to let/vacancies	* Chambres (à louer)
No vacancies	* Complet
Have you a room for the night?	Avez-vous une chambre pour une nuit?
Do you know another good hotel?	Pouvez-vous m'indiquer un autre bon hôtel?
I've reserved a room; my name is . . .	J'ai réservé une chambre; je m'appelle . . .
I want a single room with a shower	Je voudrais une chambre avec douches pour une personne
We want a room with a double bed and a bathroom	Nous voudrions une chambre avec un grand lit et salle de bain(s)
Have you a room with twin beds?	Avez-vous une chambre à deux lits?
I want a room for two or three days/for a week/until Friday	Je voudrais une chambre pour deux ou trois jours/pour une semaine/jusqu'à vendredi
What floor is the room on?	A quel étage se trouve la chambre?
Is there a lift/elevator?	Y a-t-il un ascenseur?

1. See also LAUNDRY (p. 98) and RESTAURANT (p. 65).

Have you a room on the first floor?	Avez-vous une chambre au premier étage?
May I see the room?	Pourrais-je voir la chambre?
I'll take this room	Je prends cette chambre
I don't like this room	Je n'aime pas cette chambre
Have you another one?	En avez-vous une autre?
I want a quiet room	Je veux une chambre calme
There's too much noise	Il y a trop de bruit
I'd like a room with a balcony	Je voudrais une chambre avec balcon
Have you a room looking on to the street/the sea?	Avez-vous une chambre (qui donne) sur la rue/sur la mer?
We've only a twin bedded room	* Nous n'avons qu'une chambre à deux lits
This is the only room vacant	* C'est la seule chambre libre
We shall have another room tomorrow	* Nous aurons une autre chambre demain
The room is only available tonight	* Cette chambre n'est libre que ce soir seulement
How much is the room per night?	Quel est le prix de la chambre pour une nuit?
Have you nothing cheaper?	Vous n'avez rien de moins cher?
Are service and tax included?	Est-ce que le service et la taxe sont compris?

Are meals included?	Est-ce que les repas sont compris?
How much is the room without meals?	Quel est le prix de la chambre sans repas?
How much is full board?	Quel est le prix de la chambre avec pension complète?
I'd like a room with breakfast	Je voudrais une chambre avec petit déjeuner
Do you have a weekly rate?	Avez-vous un tarif hebdomadaire?

In your room

I'd like breakfast in my room, please	Je voudrais prendre le petit déjeuner dans ma chambre, s'il vous plaît
Please wake me at 8.30	Pouvez-vous me réveiller à huit heures trente?
There's no ashtray in my room	Il n'y a pas de cendrier dans ma chambre
Can I have more hangers, please?	Pourrais-je avoir d'autres cintres, s'il vous plaît?
Is there a point for an electric razor?	Est-ce qu'il y a une prise pour rasoir électrique?

What's the voltage?[1]	Quel est le voltage?
Where is the bathroom?	Où est la salle de bains?
Where is the lavatory?	Où sont les toilettes?
Is there a shower?	Y a-t-il des douches?
There are no towels in my room	Il n'y a pas de serviette dans ma chambre
There's no soap	Il n'y a pas de savon
There's no water	Il n'y a pas d'eau
There's no plug in my washbasin	Mon lavabo n'a pas de bouchon
There's no toilet paper in the lavatory	Il n'y a pas de papier hygiénique aux toilettes
The lavatory won't flush	La chasse d'eau ne fonctionne pas
May I have the key to the bathroom, please?	Pourrais-je avoir la clé de la salle de bains?
May I have another blanket/another pillow?	Pourrais-je avoir une autre couverture/un autre oreiller?
These sheets aren't clean	Ces draps ne sont pas propres
I can't open my window, please open it	Je ne peux pas ouvrir ma fenêtre; voulez-vous l'ouvrir, s'il vous plaît
It's too hot/cold	Il fait trop chaud/froid

1. The voltage in France is 220 volts, but in some places it is still 110 volts. It is therefore important to check it, as it may vary from one place to another.

Can the heating be turned up?	Pouvez-vous chauffer davantage?
Can the heating be turned down?	Pouvez-vous baisser le chauffage?
Is the room air-conditioned?	Est-ce que la chambre est climatisée?
The air conditioning doesn't work	La climatisation ne fonctionne pas
Come in	Entrez
Put it on the table, please	Mettez cela sur la table, s'il vous plaît
I want these shoes cleaned	Je voudrais faire cirer cette paire de chaussures
I want this dress cleaned	Je voudrais faire nettoyer cette robe
I want this suit pressed	Je voudrais faire repasser ce costume
When will it be ready?	Quand est-ce que ce sera prêt?
It will be ready tomorrow	* Ce sera prêt demain

At the reception desk

My key, please	Ma clé, s'il vous plaît
Are there any letters for me?	Y a-t-il du courrier pour moi?

Is there any message for me?	Y a-t-il un message pour moi?
If anyone phones, tell them I'll be back at 4.30	Si quelqu'un téléphone, dites que je serai de retour à quatre heures et demie
No one telephoned	* Personne n'a téléphoné
There's a lady/gentleman to see you	* Une dame/un monsieur vous demande
Please ask her/him to come up	Faites la/le monter, s'il vous plaît
I'm coming down	Je descends
Have you any writing paper/envelopes/stamps?	Avez-vous du papier à lettre/des enveloppes/des timbres?
Please send the chambermaid/the waiter	Envoyez-moi la femme de chambre/le garçon, s'il vous plaît
I need a guide/an interpreter	J'ai besoin d'un guide/d'un interprète
Where is the dining room?	Où est la salle à manger?
What time is breakfast/lunch/dinner?	A quelle heure est le petit déjeuner/le déjeuner/le dîner?
Is there a garage?	Est-ce qu'il y a un garage?
Is the hotel open all night?	Est-ce que l'hôtel reste ouvert toute la nuit?
What time does it close?	A quelle heure ferme-t-il?

Departure

I have to leave tomorrow	Je dois partir demain
Can you have my bill ready?	Pouvez-vous préparer ma note?
I shall be coming back on . . ., can I book a room for that date?	Je reviendrai le . . ., pouvez-vous me réserver une chambre pour cette date?
Could you have my luggage brought down?	Pouvez-vous faire descendre mes bagages?
Please order a taxi for me at 11 a.m.	Commandez-moi un taxi pour onze heures du matin, s'il vous plaît
Thank you for a pleasant stay	Je vous remercie de votre aimable accueil

RESTAURANT

Going to a restaurant

Can you suggest a good restaurant/a cheap restaurant/ a vegetarian restaurant?	Connaissez-vous un bon restaurant/un restaurant bon marché/un restaurant végétarien?
I'd like to book a table for four at 1 p.m.	Je voudrais réserver une table pour quatre pour une heure
I've reserved a table; my name is . . .	J'ai réservé une table; je m'appelle . . .
Have you a table for three?	Avez-vous une table pour trois?
Is there a table free on the terrace?	Y a-t-il une table libre à la terrasse?
This way, please	* Par ici, s'il vous plaît
We shall have a table free in half an hour	* Il y aura une table libre dans une demi-heure
We don't serve lunch until 12	* On ne sert pas le déjeuner avant midi
We don't serve dinner until 8 p.m.	* On ne sert pas le dîner avant huit heures
We stop serving at 11 o'clock	* On ne sert plus après onze heures
Where is the cloakroom?	Où sont les toilettes?
It is downstairs	* Elles sont en bas

We are in a hurry	Nous sommes pressés
Do you serve snacks?	Est-ce que vous servez des casse-croûte?

Ordering

Service charge	* Supplément pour le service
Waiter/waitress *address*	Garçon/mademoiselle
May I see the menu/ the wine list, please?	Pourrais-je voir le menu/la carte des vins, s'il vous plaît?
Is there a set menu?	Y a-t-il un menu à prix fixe?
What do you recommend?	Qu'est-ce que vous recommandez?
Can you tell me what this is?	Pouvez-vous me dire ce que c'est?
What is the speciality of the restaurant/of the region?	Quelle est la spécialité de ce restaurant/du pays
Would you like to try . . .?	* Voulez-vous goûter . . .?
There's no more . . .	* Il n'y a plus de . . .
I'd like . . .	Je voudrais . . .
May I have peas instead of beans?	Pourrais-je avoir des petits pois à la place des haricots?
Is it hot or cold?	Est-ce chaud ou froid?

This isn't what I ordered, I want . . .	Ce n'est pas ce que j'ai commandé, je veux . . .
Without oil/sauce, please	Sans huile/sauce, s'il vous plaît
Some more bread, please	Un peu plus de pain, s'il vous plaît
A little more . . .	Un peu plus de . . .
This is bad	Ce n'est pas bon
This is uncooked	Ce n'est pas cuit
This bread is stale	Ce pain est rassis

Drinks

What will you have to drink ?	* Que désirez-vous comme boisson ?
A bottle of the local wine, please	Une bouteille de vin de la région, s'il vous plaît
Do you serve wine by the glass ?	Est-ce que vous servez du vin au verre ?
Two glasses of beer, please	Deux demis, s'il vous plaît
Do you have draught beer ?	Avez-vous de la bière à la pression ?
Two more beers, please	Encore deux demis, s'il vous plaît

I'd like another glass of water, please	Je voudrais encore un verre d'eau, s'il vous plaît
The same again, please	La même chose, s'il vous plaît
Three black coffees and one white	Trois cafés noirs et un café-crème
I want to see the head waiter	Je veux voir le maître d'hôtel
May we have an ashtray?	Pouvez-vous nous donner un cendrier?
Can I have a light, please?	Voulez-vous me donner du feu, s'il vous plaît

Paying

The bill, please	L'addition, s'il vous plaît
Does it include service?	Est-ce que le service est compris?
Please check the bill – I don't think it's correct	Voulez-vous vérifier l'addition; je crois qu'il y a une erreur
I didn't have soup	Je n'ai pas pris de soupe
I had an entrecôte, not a tournedos	J'ai pris une entrecôte, pas un tournedos
May we have separate bills?	Pouvez-vous faire l'addition séparément?

Breakfast

Breakfast[1]	Le petit déjeuner
A large white/black coffee, please	Un grand café crème/noir, s'il vous plaît
A cup of tea/chocolate, please	Une tasse de thé/chocolat, s'il vous plaît
I'd like tea with milk/lemon	Je voudrais du thé au lait/au citron
May we have some sugar, please?	Pourriez-vous nous donner du sucre, s'il vous plaît?
A roll/bread/toast and butter	Un petit pain/du pain/du pain grillé avec du beurre
Croissants (crescent-shaped rolls)	Des croissants
More butter, please	Un peu plus de beurre, s'il vous plaît
Have you some jam/marmalade?	Avez-vous de la confiture/de la confiture d'orange?
I would like a boiled egg	Je voudrais un œuf à la coque
Bacon/ham and eggs, please	Des œufs au bacon/au jambon, s'il vous plaît
What fruit juices have you?	Quelles sortes de jus de fruit avez-vous?

1. *Le petit déjeuner* (*complet*) usually consists of coffee or chocolate, rolls, croissants, and butter. It is normally the only meal taken in a café.

Restaurant vocabulary

ashtray	le cendrier
bar	le bar
beer	la bière
bill	l'addition *f*
bottle/half bottle	la bouteille/la demi-bouteille
bowl	le bol
bread	le pain
butter	le beurre
carafe	la carafe
cheese	le fromage
cigarettes	les cigarettes *f*
cloakroom	les toilettes *f*/le lavabo
coffee	le café
course (dish)	le plat
cream	la crème
cup	la tasse
fork	la fourchette
glass	le verre
hungry (to be)	(avoir) faim
knife	le couteau

lemon	le citron
matches	les allumettes *f*
mayonnaise	la mayonnaise
menu	le menu
milk	le lait
mustard	la moutarde
napkin	la serviette
oil	l'huile *f*
pepper	le poivre
plate	l'assiette *f*
restaurant	le restaurant
salt	le sel
sandwich	le sandwich
sauce	la sauce
saucer	la soucoupe
service	le service
snack	le casse-croûte
snack-bar	le snack-bar
spoon	la cuiller
sugar	le sucre
table	la table
table-cloth	la nappe
tea	le thé

terrace	la terrasse
thirsty (to be)	(avoir) soif
tip	le pourboire
toothpick	le cure-dent
vegetarian	végétarien
vinegar	le vinaigre
waiter	le garçon
waitress	la serveuse
water	l'eau *f*
wine	le vin
wine list	la carte des vins

MENU

SOUPES/POTAGES	SOUPS
Bisque	a rich soup made from shellfish (lobster, prawn bisque)
Bouillabaisse	a substantial soup made from different kinds of fish
Consommé	a clear strong beef soup
Crème vichyssoise	a cold soup made with chicken stock, leeks and cream
Petite marmite	a substantial clear soup with a predominant flavour of chicken
Potage aux champignons	mushroom soup
Potage julienne	clear soup with finely shredded vegetables
Potage parmentier	potato soup
Potage au poulet	chicken soup
Potage Saint-Germain	pea soup
Potage aux tomates	tomato soup
Soupe aux choux	cabbage soup
Soupe aux légumes	vegetable soup
Soupe à l'oignon gratinée	onion soup poured over slices of bread covered with grated cheese
Soupe de poisson	fish soup

HORS D'ŒUVRES	HORS D'ŒUVRES
Anchois	anchovy
Artichaut	artichoke
Asperges	asparagus
Cœurs d'artichaut	artichoke hearts
Cœurs de palmier	palm hearts
Confit d'oie	preserved goose
Coquilles St Jacques	scallops
Crudités	salad vegetables (tomatoes, beetroot, carrot, cucumber, etc.) with vinaigrette dressing
Escargots	snails
Foie gras truffé	goose liver pâté with truffles
Grenouilles	frogs (legs)
Huîtres	oysters
Jambon	ham
Melon	melon
Moules marinières	mussels in white wine sauce
Œuf dur mayonnaise	egg mayonnaise
Pâté (de campagne)	pâté
Quiche lorraine	a tart with a filling of egg custard, bacon, onions, and cheese
Saucisson	sausage (salami type)

Pipérade	tomatoes and peppers cooked with scrambled egg
Rillettes	a kind of potted pork, or goose and pork
Tarte à l'oignon	onion tart
Terrine (de lapin/canard)	a kind of pâté (rabbit/duck)

POISSON	FISH
Anguille	eel
Barbue	brill
Brochet	pike
Calmar	squid
Carpe	carp
Crabe	crab
Crevettes	shrimps/prawns
Colin	hake
Dorade	sea bream
Écrevisses	(freshwater) crayfish
Fruits de mer	shellfish
Hareng	herring
Homard	lobster
Homard à l'américaine	lobster in brandy with tomatoes and onions
Langouste	rock lobster

Langouste thermidor	lobster in cream sauce
Langoustines	Dublin Bay prawns/scampi
Loup de mer	sea bass
Maquereau	mackerel
Merlan	whiting
Merluche	hake
Morue (sèche)	(dried) cod
Mulet	grey mullet
Oursin	sea urchin
Palourdes	clams
Plie	plaice
Poulpe	octopus
Quenelle de brochet	a kind of dumpling made with pike
Raie	skate
Rouget	red mullet
Sardines	sardines
Saumon	salmon
Sole	sole
Sole meunière	sole cooked in butter and parsley
Thon	tunny
Truite	trout
Truite au bleu	trout cooked in vinegar flavoured stock

Truite aux amandes	trout with almonds
Turbot	turbot

VIANDE	MEAT
Bœuf:	*beef:*
Bifteck	steak
Bœuf bourguignon	beef cooked in red wine with mushrooms and onions
Bœuf en daube	beef braised in red wine and well seasoned with herbs
Carbonnades de bœuf	a rich beef stew made with beer
Châteaubriant	steak taken from the heart of a fillet of beef
Pot-au-feu	beef stewed with root vegetables
Rôti	roast
Tournedos Rossini	a thick steak cut from the eye of the fillet, with a slice of goose liver pâté
Agneau/mouton:	*lamb/mutton:*
Carré d'agneau	loin of lamb with herbs
Côtelette	chop
Épaule	shoulder
Gigot	leg

Veau:	*veal:*
Côtelette	cutlet
Escalope	escalope
Longe	loin
Poitrine	breast
Tête de veau vinaigrette	calf's head with vinaigrette sauce
Porc:	*pork:*
Basse-côtes	spare ribs
Cochon de lait	sucking pig
Côte	chop
Longe	loin
Andouilles/andouillettes	sausages made of chitterlings, usually grilled
Bacon	bacon
Boudin	black pudding or blood sausage, fried or grilled
Boulettes	meatballs/rissoles
Cervelle	brain
Choucroute garnie	sauerkraut with pork, ham, sausage, and boiled potatoes
Crépinettes	small flat sausages flavoured with herbs and brandy
Foie	liver

Jambon au madère	ham in madeira sauce
Langue	tongue
Ragoût	stew
Ris de veau	sweetbreads
Rognons	kidneys
Saucisses de Francfort/de Strasbourg	Frankfurters
Saucisses de Toulouse	big sausages with thickly cut forcemeat, grilled or fried
Tripes à la mode de Caen	tripe cooked with onions and carrots

VOLAILLE ET GIBIER	POULTRY AND GAME
Aile	wing
Blanc	breast
Canard	duck
Canard à l'orange	duck with orange sauce
Canard aux olives	duck with olives
Chevreuil	venison
Civet de lièvre	jugged hare
Coq au vin	chicken cooked in red wine with bacon, mushrooms, and onions
Cuisse	leg
Dinde	turkey

Faisan	pheasant
Lapin	rabbit
Lièvre	hare
Oie	goose
Perdreau	partridge
Pigeon	pigeon
Poule-au-pot	chicken stewed with root vegetables
Suprême	breast

LÉGUMES/SALADES	VEGETABLES/SALADS
Ail	garlic
Artichaut	artichoke
Asperges	asparagus
Aubergine	aubergine/eggplant
Betterave	beetroot
Carotte	carrot
Céleri	celery
Champignon (cèpe/morille/chanterelle)	mushroom
Chou	cabbage
Choucroute	sauerkraut
Choux de Bruxelles	Brussels sprouts

Chou-fleur	cauliflower
Concombre	cucumber
Courgette	courgette/baby marrow
Endive	chicory
Épinards	spinach
Fenouil	fennel
Fèves	broad beans
Haricots verts	green beans
Laitue	lettuce
Marrons	chestnuts
Navet	turnip
Oignon	onion
Petits pois	peas
Piment	pepper
Poireau	leek
Pommes de terre	potatoes
allumettes	chips
chips	crisps
frites	chips
en purée	creamed
Riz	rice
Tomate	tomato

ŒUFS	EGGS
A la coque	boiled
Brouillés	scrambled
Omelette	omelette
Pochés	poached
Sur le plat	fried

DESSERT	DESSERT
Beignets	fritters
Crêpes	pancakes
Crêpes Suzette	thin pancakes flamed with brandy and orange liqueur
Glaces	ices
à la vanille	vanilla
au café	coffee
au chocolat	chocolate
Granités	water ices
Omelette au rhum	rum omelette
Salade de fruits	fruit salad
Soufflé au Grand Marnier	soufflé flavoured with Grand Marnier

FRUITS ET NOIX	FRUITS AND NUTS
Abricot	apricot
Amande	almond

Ananas	pineapple
Banane	banana
Cerise	cherry
Citron	lemon
Figue	fig
Fraise	strawberry
Fraises des bois	wild strawberries
Framboise	raspberry
Groseille à maquereau	gooseberry
Orange	orange
Pamplemousse	grapefruit
Pastèque	water melon
Pêche	peach
Poire	pear
Pomme	apple
Prune	plum
Raisin	grape
Raisin sec	raisin
Reine-claude	greengage

SOME COOKING METHODS

A point	medium
Au four	baked

Bien cuit	well cooked
En cocotte	casseroled
En gelée	in aspic
Farci	stuffed
Fumé	smoked
Mornay	with cheese sauce
Persillé	with parsley
Râpé	grated
Saignant	rare

BOISSONS	DRINKS
Bière	beer
blonde	lager
brune	(brown) ale
Champagne	champagne
Cidre	cider
Cognac	brandy
Eau minérale	mineral water
Jus de fruit	fruit juice
Limonade	lemonade
Orangeade	orangeade
Porto	port
Rhum	rum
Vin de Xérès	sherry

Vin	wine
blanc	white
rosé	rosé
rouge	red
doux	sweet
sec	dry
pétillant/mousseux	sparkling

SHOPPING

Where to go

Which is the best department store?	Quel est le meilleur grand magasin?
Where is the market?	Où est le marché?
Is there a market every day?	Est-ce qu'il y a un marché tous les jours?
Where's the nearest chemist?	Où est la pharmacie la plus proche?
Can you recommend a hairdresser?	Pouvez-vous me recommander un salon de coiffure?
Where can I buy . . .?	Où puis-je acheter . . .?
When are the shops open?	Quand est-ce que les magasins sont ouverts?

In the shop

Self service	* Libre-service/self-service
Sale (clearance)	* Soldes
Cash desk	* Caisse
Shop assistant	Le vendeur/la vendeuse
Manager	Le directeur/le gérant

Can I help you?	* Vous désirez?
I want to buy . . .	Je voudrais . . .
Do you sell . . .?	Est-ce que vous avez . . .?
I'm just looking round	Je jette un coup d'œil/je regarde
I don't want to buy anything now	Je ne veux rien acheter maintenant
You'll find them at that counter	* Vous trouverez cela à ce comptoir
We've sold out but we'll have more tomorrow	* Nous n'en avons plus, mais nous en aurons d'autres demain
Will you take it with you?	* C'est pour emporter?
Please send them to this address/X hotel	Envoyez-les à cette adresse/à l'hôtel X

Choosing

What colour do you want?	* Quelle couleur désirez-vous?
I like this one	J'aime celui-ci *m*/celle-ci *f*
I prefer that one	Je préfère celui-ci *m*/celle-ci *f*
I don't like this colour	Je n'aime pas cette couleur
Have you a green one?	Est-ce que vous en avez un vert/une verte?

Do you have one in a different colour ?	Est-ce que vous en avez dans une autre couleur ?
Have you anything better ?	Avez-vous quelque chose de meilleur ?
I'd like another	J'en voudrais un (une) autre
What size ?[1]	Quelle taille/pointure ?
It's too big/too tight	C'est trop grand/trop serré
Have you a larger one/smaller one ?	En avez-vous un (une) plus grand (grande)/ un (une) plus petit (petite)
What size is this ?[1]	C'est quelle taille/pointure ?
I want size . . .	Je voudrais du . . .
The English/American size is . . .	En Angleterre/en Amérique c'est du . . .
My collar size is . . .	Je fais . . . d'encolure
My chest measurement is . . .	Je fais . . . de tour de poitrine
My waist measurement is . . .	Je fais . . . de tour de taille
What's it made of ?	En quoi est-ce ?
For how long is it guaranteed ?	Combien dure la garantie ?

1. Size = *taille* except for shoes, gloves, and hats, when *pointure* should be used. See table (p. 91) for continental sizes.

Complaints

I want to see the manager	Je veux voir le patron/le gérant
I bought this yesterday	J'ai acheté ceci hier
It doesn't work	Cela ne marche pas
This is dirty/stained/torn/ broken/cracked/bad	C'est sale/taché/déchiré/cassé/ fêlé/mauvais
Will you change it, please?	Pouvez-vous me le changer?
Will you refund my money?	Pouvez-vous me rembourser?

Paying

How much is this?	Combien coûte ceci?
That's 50 F, please	* Cela fait cinquante francs
They are one franc each	* Ils/elles coûtent un franc pièce
It's too expensive	C'est trop cher
Don't you have anything cheaper?	Vous n'avez rien de moins cher?
Will you take English/ American currency?	Acceptez-vous l'argent anglais/ les dollars?
Do you take travellers' cheques?	Acceptez-vous les chèques de voyage?

Do you give any discount?	Est-ce que vous faites une remise?
Please pay the cashier	* Payez à la caisse, s'il vous plaît
May I have a receipt, please?	Pourriez-vous me donner un reçu?
You've given me the wrong change	Vous vous êtes trompé en me rendant la monnaie

Clothes and shoes[1]

I want a hat/sunhat	Je voudrais un chapeau/un chapeau de paille
I'd like a pair of white cotton gloves/black leather gloves	Je voudrais une paire de gants blancs en coton/une paire de gants en cuir noir
May I see some dresses, please?	Pourrais-je voir des robes, s'il vous plaît?
I like the one in the window	J'aime celle qui est en vitrine
May I try this?	Puis-je essayer celle-ci?
That's smart	C'est très élégant
It doesn't fit me	Cela ne me va pas bien
I don't like this style	Je n'aime pas ce genre
Where's the coat department?	Où est le rayon des manteaux?
Where are beach clothes?	Où sont les vêtements pour la plage?

1. For sizes see p. 91.

The fashion department is on the second floor	* Le rayon des modes est au deuxième étage
I want a short/long sleeved shirt, collar size . . .	Je voudrais une chemise à manches courtes/ longues, . . . d'encolure
A pair of grey wool socks, please, size 10	Une paire de chaussettes de laine grise, s'il vous plaît, trent-neuf de pointure
I need a pair of walking shoes	Je voudrais une paire de chaussures pour la marche
I need a pair of beach sandals/ black shoes	Je désire une paire de sandales pour la plage/de chaussures noires
These heels are too high/too low	Ces talons sont trop hauts/trop courts

Clothing sizes

These tables are intended only as a rough guide since sizes vary from manufacturer to manufacturer.

WOMEN'S DRESSES, ETC.

British	32	34	36	38	40	42	44
American	10	12	14	16	18	20	22
French	38	40	42	44	46	48	50

MEN'S SUITS

British and American	36	38	40	42	44	46
Continental	46	48	50	52	54	56

MEN'S SHIRTS

British and American	14	14½	15	15½	16	16½	17
Continental	36	37	38	39	41	42	43

STOCKINGS

British and American	8	8½	9	9½	10	10½	11
Continental	0	1	2	3	4	5	6

SOCKS

British and American	9½	10	10½	11	11½
Continental	38–39	39–40	40–41	41–42	42–43

SHOES

British	1	2	3	4	5	6	7	8	9	10
American	2½	3½	4½	5½	6½	7½	8½	9½	10½	11½
Continental	33	34–35	36	37	38	39–40	41	42	43	44

British	11	12
American	12½	13½
Continental	45	46

Chemist[1]

Can you prepare this prescription for me, please?	Pouvez-vous me préparer cette ordonnance, s'il vous plaît?
Have you a small first aid kit?	Avez-vous une petite trousse de secours?
A tube of aspirin, please	Un tube d'aspirine, s'il vous plaît
A tin of adhesive plaster	Une boîte de sparadrap
Can you suggest something for indigestion/constipation/diarrhoea?	Pouvez-vous me recommander quelque chose pour le mal d'estomac/pour la constipation/pour la diarrhée?
I want something for insect bites	Je voudrais quelque chose contre les piqûres d'insectes
Can you give me something for sunburn?	Pouvez-vous me donner quelque chose pour les coups de soleil?
I want some throat lozenges	Je voudrais des pastilles pour la gorge

1. See also At the Doctor's (p. 118).

Toilet requisites

A packet of razor blades, please	Un paquet de lames de rasoir, s'il vous plaît
How much is this after-shave lotion?	Combien coûte cette lotion après-rasage?
A tube of toothpaste, please	Un tube de pâte dentifrice, s'il vous plaît
A box of paper handkerchiefs, please	Une boîte de mouchoirs en papier, s'il vous plaît
I want some eau-de-cologne/perfume	Je voudrais de l'eau-de-cologne/du parfum
May I try it?	Puis-je l'essayer?
What kinds of toilet soap have you?	Quelles marques de savonnettes avez-vous?
A bottle/tube of shampoo, please, for dry/greasy hair	Un flacon/un tube de shampooing pour cheveux secs/gras

Photography

I want to buy a camera	Je voudrais acheter un appareil photographique

Have you a film for this camera?	Avez-vous des pellicules pour cet appareil?
A 120 . . . film, please	Une pellicule de cent-vingt, s'il vous plaît
Give me a 35 mm. film with 20/36 exposures	Donnez-moi un film de trente-cinq millimètres, vingt/trente-six poses
Would you fit the film in the camera for me, please?	Pouvez-vous charger l'appareil, s'il vous plaît?
How much is it?	C'est combien?
Does the price include processing?	Est-ce que le développement est compris dans le prix?
I'd like this film developed and printed	Je voudrais faire développer et tirer ce film
Please enlarge this negative	Pouvez-vous agrandir ce négatif, s'il vous plaît
When will it be ready?	Quand est-ce que ce sera prêt?
Will it be done tomorrow?	Est-ce que ce sera fait demain?
My camera's not working, can you mend it?	Mon appareil ne marche pas, pouvez-vous le réparer?
The film is jammed	La pellicule est bloquée

Food[1]

Give me a kilo/half a kilo (pound) of . . ., please	Donnez-moi un kilo/un demi-kilo (une livre) de . . ., s'il vous plaît
100 grammes of sweets/chocolate, please	Cent grammes de bonbons/de chocolat, s'il vous plaît
A bottle of milk/wine/beer, please	Une bouteille de lait/vin/bière, s'il vous plaît
Is there anything back on the bottle?	Est-ce que la bouteille est consignée?
I want a jar/tin/can/packet of . . .	Je voudrais un pot/une boîte/un paquet de . . .
Do you sell frozen foods?	Vendez-vous des aliments surgelés?
These pears are too hard	Ces poires sont trop dures
Is it fresh?	Est-ce frais?
Are they ripe?	Sont-elles mûres?
This is bad	C'est mauvais
This is stale	Ce n'est pas frais
A loaf of bread, please[2]	Un pain, s'il vous plaît

1. See also RESTAURANT (p. 65) and WEIGHTS AND MEASURES (p. 131).
2. French loaves:
   une flute – a small thin stick.
   une baguette – a longer, slightly thicker stick (the most common French bread).
   un bâtard – shorter and thicker than a *baguette*.
   un pain de mie – English loaf.

How much a kilo/bottle?	Combien est-ce le kilo/la bouteille?

Tobacconist[1]

Do you stock English/American cigarettes?	Avez-vous des cigarettes anglaises/américaines?
What cigarettes have you?	Quelles marques de cigarettes avez-vous?
A packet of . . ., please	Un paquet de . . ., s'il vous plaît
I want some filter tip cigarettes/cigarettes without filter/mentholated cigarettes	Je voudrais des cigarettes à bout filtre/des cigarettes sans filtre/des cigarettes mentholées
A box of matches, please	Une boîte d'allumettes, s'il vous plaît
I want to buy a lighter	Je voudrais acheter un briquet
Do you sell lighter fuel?	Vendez-vous de l'essence pour briquet?
I want a gas refill for this lighter	Je voudrais une recharge de gaz pour ce briquet

1. Tobacconists in France also sell postage stamps.

Newspapers, books, writing materials

Do you sell English/American newspapers?	Avez-vous des journaux anglais/américains?
Can you get . . . for me?	Pourriez-vous faire venir . . . pour moi?
Where can I get the . . .?	Où pourrais-je trouver le . . .?
I want a map of the city	Je voudrais un plan de la ville
I want an entertainment/amusements guide[1]	Je voudrais un guide des spectacles
Do you have any English books?	Avez-vous des livres anglais?
Have you any books by . . .?	Avez-vous des livres de . . .?
I want some coloured postcards/black and white postcards	Je voudrais des cartes postales en couleurs/des cartes postales en noir et blanc

Laundry and cleaning

I want to have these things washed/cleaned	Je voudrais faire laver/faire nettoyer ces affaires
It only needs to be pressed	Ceci n'a besoin que d'être repassé

1. In Paris, the equivalent to *What's on in London* is called *La semaine de Paris.*

This is torn; can you mend it?	Ceci est déchiré; pouvez-vous le réparer?
Do you do invisible mending?	Est-ce que vous faites le stoppage?
There's a button missing	Il manque un bouton
Will you sew on another one, please?	Pouvez-vous le remplacer, s'il vous plaît?
When will it be ready?	Quand est-ceque ce sera prêt?
I need them by this evening/ tomorrow	J'en ai besoin pour ce soir/pour demain
Call back at 5 o'clock	* Revenez vers cinq heures
We can't do it before Tuesday	* Nous ne pouvons pas le faire avant mardi
It will take three days	* Cela prendra trois jours

Repairs

SHOES

I want these shoes soled	Je voudrais faire ressemeler ces chaussures
I want leather soles	Je voudrais des semelles en cuir
I want these shoes heeled with rubber	Je voudrais faire mettre des talons en caoutchouc à cette paire de chaussures

I have broken the heel; can you put on a new one?	J'ai cassé le talon; pouvez-vous le remplacer?
Can you do them while I wait?	Pouvez-vous les réparer tout de suite?
When should I pick them up?	Quand dois-je passer les prendre?

WATCH/JEWELLERY

My watch is broken	Ma montre est cassée
My watch is always fast/slow	Ma montre prend de l'avance/du retard
Can you repair it?	Pouvez-vous la réparer?
I've broken the strap	J'ai cassé le bracelet
The fastener is broken	Le fermoir est cassé
The stone is loose	La pierre bouge
How much will it cost?	Combien est-ce que cela coûtera?
It can't be repaired	* C'est irréparable
You need a new watch/strap	* Vous avez besoin d'une nouvelle montre/un nouveau bracelet

BARBER AND HAIRDRESSER

May I make an appointment for this morning/tomorrow afternoon ?	Pourrais-je prendre un rendez-vous pour ce matin/pour demain après-midi ?
What time ?	A quelle heure ?
I want my hair cut	Je voudrais me faire couper les cheveux
Just a trim, please	Simplement rafraîchir, s'il vous plaît
Not too short at the sides	Pas trop courts sur le côté
I'll have it shorter at the back, please	Je les voudrais un peu plus courts derrière, s'il vous plaît
This is where I have my parting	C'est là que je fais la raie
My hair is oily/dry	Mes cheveux sont gras/secs
I want a shampoo	Je voudrais un shampooing
I want my hair washed and set	Je voudrais un shampooing-mise en plis
Please set it without rollers/ on large/small rollers	Une mise en plis sans rouleaux/ avec gros/petits rouleaux, s'il vous plaît
I want a colour rinse	Je voudrais un rinçage
I'd like to see a colour chart	Puis-je voir la gamme des coloris ?
I want a darker/lighter shade	Je voudrais une teinte plus foncée/plus claire
I want my hair bleached	Je voudrais me faire décolorer les cheveux

I want a tint/a perm	Je voudrais un colorant/une permanente
Have you any lacquer?	Avez-vous de la laque?
The water is too cold	L'eau est trop froide
The dryer is too hot	Le séchoir est trop chaud
Thank you, I like it very much	Merci, c'est très bien
I want a manicure	Je voudrais me faire faire les mains

POST OFFICE

Where's the main post office ?	Où est le bureau de poste principal ?
Where's the nearest post office ?	Où est le bureau de poste le plus proche ?
What time does the post office close ?	À quelle heure ferme le bureau de poste ?
Where's the post box ?	Où est la boîte aux lettres ?

Letters and telegrams[1]

How much is a postcard to England ?	A combien faut-il affranchir une carte postale pour l'Angleterre ?
What's the airmail to the USA. ?	A combien faut-il affranchir une lettre avion pour les Etats-Unis ?
How much is it to send a letter surface mail to the USA ?	A combien faut-il affranchir une lettre pour les Etats-Unis par la voie ordinaire ?
It's for France	C'est pour la France
Give me three 30 centimes stamps, please	Donnez-moi trois timbres à trente centimes, s'il vous plaît

1. In France stamps are on sale in tobacconists and newsagents as well as in post offices. In the Paris postal region an express letter (*un pneumatique*) can be sent by pneumatic tube from any post office.

I want to send this letter express	Je voudrais envoyer cette lettre exprès
I want to register this letter	Je voudrais recommander cette lettre
Where is the poste restante section?	Où est le guichet de la poste restante?
Are there any letters for me?	Y a-t-il du courrier pour moi?
What is your name?	* Comment vous appelez-vous?
Have you any means of identification?	* Avez-vous une pièce d'identité?
I want to send a (reply paid) telegram	Je voudrais envoyer un télégramme (réponse payée)
How much does it cost per word?	C'est combien le mot?
Write the message here and your own name and address	* Ecrivez le texte ici et mettez votre nom et adresse

Telephoning[1]

Where's the nearest phone box?	Où est la cabine téléphonique la plus proche?

1. Telephone boxes are found in post offices and most public places, e.g. stations; there are also a few in the street. Most cafés have public telephones and it is quite usual to telephone from there. Many call boxes require special tokens (*jetons*) for

I want to make a phone call	Je voudrais donner un coup de téléphone
Please give me a token	Donnez-moi un jeton, s'il vous plaît
Please get me Invalides 27-83[1]	Donnez-moi Invalides 27-83 (vingt-sept, quatre-vingt trois)
I want to telephone to England	Je voudrais téléphoner en Angleterre
I want to reverse the charges/ call collect	Je voudrais une communication en p.c.v.
Hallo	Allô
I want extension 43	Je voudrais le poste quarante-trois
May I speak to . . .	Pourrais-je parler à . . .
Who's speaking?	* Qui est à l'appareil, s'il vous plaît?
Hold the line, please	* Ne quittez pas
Put the receiver down	* Raccrochez
He's not here	* Il n'est pas là
He's at . . .	* Il est à . . .
When will he be back?	Quand sera-t-il de retour?
Will you take a message?	Voulez-vous prendre un message?

local calls; these can be bought at the post office, or in the café. To make a long distance call you must go to a post office or large café where there is a switchboard, or telephone from a private number, e.g. your hotel.

1. French telephone numbers are always given in sets of two figures (e.g. 27–83).

Tell him that X phoned	Dites-lui que X a téléphoné
I'll ring again later	Je rappellerai plus tard
Please ask him to phone me	Demandez-lui de me rappeler, s'il vous plaît
What's your number	* Quel est votre numéro ?
My number is . . .	Mon numéro est . . .
I can't hear you	Je vous entends très mal
The line is engaged	* La ligne est occupée
There's no reply	* Il n'y a pas de réponse/le numéro ne répond pas
You have the wrong number	* Vous vous êtes trompé de numéro

SIGHTSEEING[1]

What ought one to see here?	Que faut-il visiter ici?
What's this building?	Qu'est-ce que ce bâtiment?
Which is the oldest building in the city?	Quel est le plus vieux monument de la ville?
When was it built?	Quand a-t-il été construit?
Who built it?	Qui l'a construit?
What's the name of this church?	Comment s'appelle cette église?
What time is mass/the service at . . . church?	A quelle heure a lieu la messe/ l'office à l'église . . . ?
Is there an English church/ a synagogue?	Y a-t-il une église anglaise/ une synagogue?
Please cover your head	* Couvrez-vous, s'il vous plaît
Is this the natural history museum?	Est-ce bien le muséum d'histoire naturelle?
When is the museum open?	Quelles sont les heures d'ouverture du musée?
Is it open on Sundays?	Est-il ouvert le dimanche?
The museum is closed on Tuesdays[2]	* Le musée est fermé le mardi
Admission free	* Entrée libre/gratuite

1. See also BUS and COACH TRAVEL (p. 43), DIRECTIONS (p. 46).

2. Most Paris museums open at 10 a.m. and close at 5 p.m.; elsewhere the hours are likely to be 10 to noon and 2 to 5 p.m. In and around Paris Tuesday is the usual closing day; in other cities it is Monday.

How much is it to go in?	Combien coûte l'entrée?
Have you a ticket?	* Avez-vous un billet?
Where do I get tickets?	Où achète-t-on les billets?
Please leave your bag in the cloakroom	* Veuillez déposer votre sac au vestiaire
It's over there	* C'est là-bas
Can I take pictures?	Est-ce que je peux prendre des photos?
Cameras are prohibited	* Les appareils de photo sont interdits
Follow the guide	* Suivez le guide
Does the guide speak English?	Est-ce que le guide parle anglais?
We don't need a guide	Nous n'avons pas besoin de guide
Where is the X collection/exhibition?	Où se trouve la collection/l'exposition X?
Where are the Rembrandts?	Où sont les Rembrandt?
Where can I get a catalogue?	Où puis-je me procurer un catalogue?
Where can I get a plan/guide book of the city?	Où puis-je trouver un plan/un guide de la ville?
Is this the way to the zoo?	Est-ce la bonne direction pour aller au zoo?
Which bus goes to the castle?	Quel autobus va au château?

How do I get to the park?	Comment puis-je me rendre au parc?
Can we walk it?	Pouvons-nous y aller à pied?

ENTERTAINMENT

What's on at the theatre/ cinema ?[1]	Qu'est-ce qu'on joue au théâtre/ au cinéma ?
Is there a concert ?	Est-ce qu'il y a un concert ?
I want two seats for tonight/ for the matinée tomorrow	Je voudrais deux places pour ce soir/pour la matinée de demain
I want to book seats for Thursday	Je voudrais louer des places pour jeudi
Are they good seats ?	Est-ce que ce sont de bonnes places ?
Where are these seats ?	Où sont ces places ?
When does the curtain go up ?	Le lever du rideau est à quelle heure ?
What time does the performance end ?	A quelle heure finit le spectacle ?
A programme please	Un programme, s'il vous plaît
What's the best nightclub ?	Quel est le meilleur cabaret/ nightclub ?
What time is the floorshow ?	A quelle heure commencent les attractions ?

1. Theatres always close one day each week, but are open for the matinée performance on Sundays. Seats can be reserved at the theatre every day from 11 a.m. to 5 p.m.; they are normally only on sale about a week before any given performance. Cinemas in Paris and other large French cities are open from 2 p.m. to midnight. Many have set hours for performances, the others are *cinémas permanents* – i.e. performances are continuous.

May I have this dance?	Voulez-vous m'accorder cette danse? *more familiar:* Vous dansez, mademoiselle?
Is there a jazz club here?	Y a-t-il un club de jazz ici?
Do you have a discotheque here?	Y a-t-il une discothèque ici?

SPORTS AND GAMES

Where is the stadium?	Où est le stade?
Are there any seats left in the grandstand?	Reste-t-il des places aux tribunes?
How much are the cheapest seats?	Combien valent les places les moins chères?
Are the seats in the sun/shade?	Y a-t-il des places au soleil/à l'ombre?
We want to go to a football match/the tennis tournament/a bullfight	Nous voulons aller voir un match de football/le tournoi de tennis/une course de taureaux
Who's playing?	Qui est-ce qui joue?
When does it start?	A quelle heure est-ce que cela commence?
What is the score?	Quel est le score (*rugby and soccer*)/Où en est la partie? (*tennis*)
Who's winning?	Qui gagne?
Where's the race course?	Où est le champ de courses/l'hippodrome?
When's the next meeting?	Quand a lieu la prochaine réunion?
Which is the favourite?	Quel est le favori?
Who's the jockey?	Qui est le jockey?

10 francs to win on . . .[1]	Dix francs gagnant sur . . .
10 francs each way on . . .	Dix francs gagnant, dix francs placé sur . . .
What are the odds?	Quelle est la cote?

1. The equivalent of the tote in France is the P.M.U. (Pari Mutuel Urbain). Bets can be placed at the offices at a race course or at any café or tobacconist with the sign P.M.U.

ON THE BEACH

Which is the best beach ?	Quelle est la meilleure plage ?
Is there a quiet beach near here ?	Y a-t-il une plage tranquille près d'ici ?
Is it far to walk ?	Est-ce loin à pied ?
Is there a bus to the beach ?	Y a-t-il un autobus qui va à la plage ?
Is the beach sand or shingle ?	Est-ce une plage de sable ou de galets ?
Is the bathing dangerous from this beach/bay ?	Est-ce qu'il est dangereux de se baigner sur cette plage/dans cette baie ?
Bathing prohibited	* Baignade interdite
It's dangerous	* C'est dangereux
Is the tide rising/falling ?	Est-ce que la marée monte/descend ?
There's a strong current here	* Le courant est violent ici
You will be out of your depth	* Vous n'aurez pas pied
Are you a strong swimmer ?	* Êtes-vous bon nageur ?
Is it deep ?	Est-ce que c'est profond ?
How's the water ? Cold ?	Est-ce que l'eau est froide ?
It's warm	Elle est chaude/bonne
Can one swim in the lake/river ?[1]	Peut-on se baigner dans le lac/le fleuve/la rivière ?

1. There are two words for 'river' in French. *Fleuve* is used for rivers that flow into the sea and *rivière* for rivers that flow into *fleuves*.

Is there an indoor/outdoor swimming pool?	Y a-t-il une piscine couverte/en plein air?
Is it salt or fresh water?	Est-ce de l'eau salée ou de l'eau douce?
Are there showers?	Y a-t-il des douches?
I want to hire a cabin for the day/morning/two hours	Je voudrais louer une cabine pour la journée/pour la matinée/pour deux heures
I want to hire a deckchair/sunshade	Je voudrais louer une chaise longue/un parasol
Can we water ski here?	Peut-on faire du ski nautique ici?
Can we hire the equipment?	Peut-on louer l'équipement?
Where's the harbour?	Où est le port?
Can we go out in a fishing boat?	Peut-on aller faire une promenade en bateau de pêche?
We want to go fishing	Nous voudrions aller à la pêche
Is there any underwater fishing?	Est-ce qu'on fait de la pêche sous-marine ici?
Can I hire a rowing boat/motor boat?	Peut-on louer un bateau à rames/un canot à moteur?
What does it cost by the hour?	Combien coûte l'heure de location?

CAMPING AND WALKING[1]

How long is the walk to the Youth Hostel?	Combien de temps faut-il pour aller à l'Auberge de Jeunesse à pied?
How far is the next village?	A quelle distance se trouve le prochain village?
Is there a footpath to ...?	Y a-t-il un sentier qui mène à ...?
Is it possible to go there across country?	Est-il possible d'y aller à travers champs?
Is there a short cut?	Y a-t-il un raccourci?
It's an hour's walk to ...	* Il faut une heure de marche pour aller à ...
Is there a camping site near here?	Y a-t-il un terrain de camping près d'ici?
Is this an authorized camp site?	Est-ce un terrain de camping officiel?
Is drinking water/are sanitary arrangements/showers provided?	Y a-t-il de l'eau potable/des aménagements sanitaires/des douches?
May we camp here?	Pouvons-nous camper ici?
Can we hire a tent?	Peut-on louer une tente?
Can we park our caravan here?	Peut-on garer la caravane ici?
Is this drinking water?	Est-ce que cette eau est potable?
Where are the shops?	Où sont les magasins?

1. See also DIRECTIONS (p. 46).

Where can I buy paraffin/ butane gas?	Où puis-je acheter du pétrole/ du gaz butane?
May we light a fire?	Pouvons-nous faire du feu?
Where do I dispose of rubbish?	Où puis-je vider les ordures?

AT THE DOCTOR'S

I must see a doctor, can you recommend one?	Il faut que je consulte un médecin; pouvez-vous m'en recommander un?
Please call a doctor	Faites venir un médecin, s'il vous plaît
I am ill	Je suis malade
I've a pain in my right arm	J'ai une douleur au bras droit
My wrist hurts	Mon poignet me fait mal
I think I've sprained/broken my ankle	Je crois que je me suis foulé/cassé la cheville
I fell down and hurt my back	Je suis tombé et je me suis fait mal au dos
My foot is swollen	Mon pied est enflé
I've burned/cut/hurt myself	Je me suis brûlé/coupé/fait mal
My stomach[1] is upset	J'ai mal au ventre
I have indigestion	J'ai mal à l'estomac/je digère mal
My appetite's gone	Je n'ai plus d'appétit
I think I've got food poisoning	Je crois souffrir d'une intoxication alimentaire
I can't eat/sleep	Je ne peux pas manger/dormir
I am a diabetic	Je suis diabétique
My nose keeps bleeding	Je saigne constamment du nez

1. 'Stomach' in English is used loosely to apply to the abdomen. The French word *estomac* has a stricter anatomical meaning.

I have earache	J'ai mal à l'oreille (*one ear*)/ aux oreilles (*both*)
I have difficulty in breathing	J'ai du mal à respirer
I feel dizzy	J'ai des vertiges
I feel sick	J'ai des nausées
I keep vomiting	Je vomis souvent
I think I've caught 'flu	Je crois que j'ai attrapé la grippe
I've got a cold	Je suis enrhumé
I've had it since yesterday/for a few hours	Je le suis depuis hier/depuis quelques heures
You're hurting me	Vous me faites mal
Must I stay in bed?	Dois-je garder le lit?
Will you call again?	Est-ce que vous repasserez me voir?
How much do I owe you?	Combien vous dois-je?
When can I travel again?	Quand pourrai-je repartir?
I feel better now	Je me sens mieux maintenant
Where does it hurt?	* Où avez-vous mal?
Have you a pain here?	* Avez-vous mal là?
How long have you had the pain?	* Depuis quand avez-vous cette douleur?
Open your mouth	* Ouvrez la bouche
Put out your tongue	* Montrez-moi votre langue

Breathe in	* Respirez/inspirez
Breathe out	* Soufflez/expirez
Does that hurt?	* Est-ce que cela vous fait mal?
A lot?	* Très mal?
A little?	* Un peu?
Please lie down	* Allongez-vous, s'il vous plaît
I'll give you some pills/medicine	* Je vais vous donner des pilules/ des médicaments
Take this prescription to the chemist's	* Allez chez le pharmacien avec cette ordonnance
Take this three times a day	* Prenez ceci trois fois par jour
I'll give you an injection	* Je vais vous faire une piqûre
Roll up your sleeve	* Retroussez votre manche
I'll put you on a diet	* Je vais vous mettre au régime
Come and see me again in two days' time	* Revenez me voir dans deux jours
Your leg must be X-rayed	* Il faut faire radiographier votre jambe
You must go to hospital	* Il faut que vous alliez à l'hôpital
You must stay in bed	* Vous devez rester au lit

AT THE DENTIST'S

I must see a dentist	Je dois voir un dentiste
Can I make an appointment with the dentist?	Puis-je prendre rendez-vous avec le dentiste?
As soon as possible	Le plus tôt possible
I have toothache	J'ai mal aux dents
This tooth hurts	Cette dent me fait mal
I've lost a filling	J'ai perdu un plombage
Can you fill it?	Pouvez-vous la plomber?
Can you do it now?	Pouvez-vous le faire maintenant?
Will you take the tooth out?	Allez-vous m'arracher la dent?
Please give me an injection first	Insensibilisez-moi la dent d'abord, s'il vous plaît
My gums are swollen	Mes gencives sont enflées
My gums keep bleeding	Mes gencives saignent souvent
I've broken my plate; can you repair it?	J'ai cassé mon dentier; pouvez-vous le réparer?
You're hurting me	Vous me faites mal
How much do I owe you?	Combien vous dois-je?
When should I come again?	Quand dois-je revenir?
Please rinse your mouth	* Rincez-vous la bouche, s'il vous plaît
I will X-ray your teeth	* Je vais prendre une radio de vos dents

You have an abscess	* Vous avez un abcès
The nerve is exposed	* Le nerf est à vif
This tooth can't be saved	* Cette dent est perdue

PROBLEMS AND ACCIDENTS

Where's the police station?[1]	Où est le commissariat de police/ la gendarmerie?
Call the police	Appelez la police
Where is the British consulate?	Où est le consulat britannique?
Please let the consulate know	Veuillez informer le consulat, s'il vous plaît
My bag has been stolen	On m'a volé mon sac
I found this in the street	J'ai trouvé ceci dans la rue
I have lost my luggage/ passport/traveller's cheques	J'ai perdu mes bagages/mon passeport/mes chèques de voyage
I have missed my train	J'ai manqué le train
My luggage is on board	Mes bagages sont à bord
Call a doctor	Appelez un médecin
Call an ambulance	Appelez une ambulance
There has been an accident[2]	Il y a eu un accident
He's badly hurt	Il est gravement blessé
He has fainted	Il s'est évanoui

1. In towns and cities police duties are performed by *agents* (*de police*), addressed as *Monsieur l'agent*. The police station is called *commissariat de police*. In very small towns and in the country police duties are performed by *gendarmes* and the police station is called the *gendarmerie*. There is a special police branch whose main duty is to patrol the roads and enforce traffic regulations. This is known as *la police de la route* and the policemen are familiarly known as *motards*.

2. If you are involved in an accident in a town get the *agent de police* to make a report (*dresser un constat*). In the country if there has been injury to people, advise the *gendarmerie*. In other cases engage a *huissier* (sheriff's officer) from the nearest town to make a report. Try to get the names and addresses of witnesses.

He's losing blood	Il perd du sang
Please get some water/a blanket/ some bandages	Allez chercher un peu d'eau/ une couverture/des pansements, s'il vous plaît
I've broken my glasses	J'ai cassé mes lunettes
I can't see	Je ne vois pas
A child has fallen in the water	Un enfant est tombé dans l'eau
A woman is drowning	Il y a une femme qui se noie
May I see your insurance policy?	* Je voudrais voir votre police d'assurance
Apply to the insurance company	Adressez-vous à la compagnie d'assurances
I want a copy of the police report	Je voudrais une copie du constat
There's a bus strike	* Il y a une grève des autobus

TIME AND DATES

What time is it?	Quelle heure est-il?
It's one o'clock	Il est une heure
two o'clock	deux heures
midday	midi
midnight	minuit
quarter to ten	dix heures moins le quart
quarter past five	cinq heures et quart
half past four	quatre heures et demie
five past eight	huit heures cinq
twenty to three	trois heures moins vingt
twenty-five to seven	sept heures moins vingt-cinq
twenty-five past eight	huit heures vingt-cinq
It's early/late	Il est tôt/tard
My watch is slow/fast/has stopped	Ma montre retarde/avance/s'est arrêtée
What time does it start/finish?	A quelle heure est-ce que cela commence/finit?
Are you staying long?	Comptez-vous rester longtemps?
I'm staying for 2 weeks/four days	Je pense rester deux semaines/quatre jours
I've been here for a week	Je suis ici depuis une semaine
We're leaving on January 5th[1]	Nous partons le cinq janvier
We got here on July 27th	Nous sommes arrivés le vingt-sept juillet

1. In French, cardinal numbers are used for dates except for the first, for which *premier* is used.

What's the date?	Quelle est la date?
It's December 9th	Nous sommes le neuf décembre
Today	aujourd'hui
Yesterday	hier
Tomorrow	demain
Day after tomorrow	après-demain
Day before yesterday	avant-hier
Day	le jour/la journée
Morning	le matin/la matinée
Afternoon	l'après-midi *m*
Evening	le soir/la soirée
Night	la nuit
This morning	ce matin
Yesterday afternoon	hier après-midi
Tomorrow evening	demain soir
In the morning	dans la matinée
In ten days' time	dans dix jours
On Tuesday	mardi
On Sundays	le dimanche
This week	cette semaine
Last month	le mois dernier
Next year	l'année prochaine
Sunday	dimanche

Monday	lundi
Tuesday	mardi
Wednesday	mercredi
Thursday	jeudi
Friday	vendredi
Saturday	samedi

January	janvier
February	février
March	mars
April	avril
May	mai
June	juin
July	juillet
August	août
September	septembre
October	octobre
November	novembre
December	décembre

PUBLIC HOLIDAYS

IN FRANCE

1 January
Easter Monday – Lundi de Pâques
1 May (Labour Day) – Fête du Travail
Ascension Day – L'Ascension (6th Thursday after Easter)
Whit Monday – Lundi de Pentecôte
14 July (Bastille Day) – Fête Nationale
15 August (The Assumption) – L'Assomption
1 November (All Saints Day) – La Toussaint
11 November
25 December

IN BELGIUM

1 January
Easter Monday
1 May
Ascension Day
Whit Monday
21 July
15 August
1 November
11 November
15 November
25 December

IN SWITZERLAND

1 January
Good Friday – Vendredi Saint
Easter Monday
Whit Monday
25 December

NUMBERS

CARDINAL

0 zéro
1 un
2 deux
3 trois
4 quatre
5 cinq
6 six
7 sept
8 huit
9 neuf
10 dix
11 onze
12 douze
13 treize
14 quatorze
15 quinze
16 seize
17 dix-sept
18 dix-huit
19 dix-neuf
20 vingt
21 vingt et un
22 vingt-deux
30 trente
31 trente et un
32 trente-deux
40 quarante
41 quarante et un
42 quarante-deux
50 cinquante
51 cinquante et un
52 cinquante-deux
60 soixante
61 soixante et un
62 soixante-deux
70 soixante-dix
71 soixante et onze
72 soixante-douze
80 quatre-vingts
81 quatre-vingt-un
82 quatre-vingt-deux
90 quatre-vingt-dix
91 quatre-vingt-onze
92 quatre-vingt-douze

100	cent	15th	quinzième
101	cent un	16th	seizième
200	deux cents	17th	dix-septième
1000	mille	18th	dix-huitième
2000	deux mille	19th	dix-neuvième
1,000,000	un million	20th	vingtième
		21st	vingt et unième
ORDINAL		30th	trentième
1st	premier	40th	quarantième
2nd	deuxième/second	50th	cinquantième
3rd	troisième	60th	soixantième
4th	quatrième	70th	soixante-dixième
5th	cinquième	80th	quatre-vingtième
6th	sixième	90th	quatre-vingt-dixième
7th	septième	100th	centième
8th	huitième		
9th	neuvième		
10th	dixième	half	demi
11th	onzième	quarter	quart
12th	douzième	three quarters	trois quarts
13th	treizième	a third	un tiers
14th	quatorzième	two thirds	deux tiers

In Belgium and Switzerland *septante, octante, nonante* = 70, 80, 90 with the intervening numbers corresponding.

WEIGHTS AND MEASURES

Distance: kilometres – miles

km.	*miles or km.*	miles	km.	*miles or km.*	miles
1·6	*1*	0·6	14·5	*9*	5·6
3·2	*2*	1·2	16·1	*10*	6·2
4·8	*3*	1·9	32·2	*20*	12·4
6·4	*4*	2·5	40·2	*25*	15·3
8	*5*	3·1	80·5	*50*	31·1
9·7	*6*	3·7	160·9	*100*	62·1
11·3	*7*	4·4	804·7	*500*	310·7
12·9	*8*	5·0			

A rough way to convert from miles to km.: divide by 5 and multiply by 8; from km. to miles: divide by 8 and multiply by 5.

Length and height: centimetres – inches

cm.	*inch or cm.*	inch	cm.	*inch or cm.*	inch
2·5	*1*	0·4	17·8	*7*	2·8
5·1	*2*	0·8	20	*8*	3·2
7·6	*3*	1·2	22·9	*9*	3·5
10·2	*4*	1·6	25·4	*10*	3·9

cm.	*inch or cm.*	inch	cm.	*inch or cm.*	inch
12·7	*5*	2·0	50·8	*20*	9·9
15·2	*6*	2·4	127	*50*	19·7

A rough way to convert from inches to cm.: divide by 2 and multiply by 5; from cm. to inches: divide by 5 and multiply by 2.

metres – feet

m.	*ft or m.*	ft	m.	*ft or m.*	ft
0·3	*1*	3·3	2·4	*8*	26·3
0·6	*2*	6·6	2·7	*9*	29·5
0·9	*3*	9·8	3	*10*	32·8
1·2	*4*	13·1	6·1	*20*	65·6
1·5	*5*	16·4	15·2	*50*	164
1·8	*6*	19·7	30·5	*100*	328·1
2·1	*7*	23			

A rough way to convert from ft to m.: divide by 10 and multiply by 3; from m. to ft: divide by 3 and multiply by 10.

metres – yards

m.	*yds or m.*	yds	m.	*yds or m.*	yds
0·9	*1*	1·1	7·3	*8*	8·8
1·8	*2*	2·2	8·2	*9*	9·8
2·7	*3*	3·3	9·1	*10*	10·9
3·7	*4*	4·4	18·3	*20*	21·9
4·6	*5*	5·5	45·7	*50*	54·7
5·5	*6*	6·6	91·4	*100*	109·4
6·4	*7*	7·7	457·2	*500*	546·8

A rough way to convert from yds to m.: subtract 10 per cent from the number of yds; from m. to yds: add 10 per cent to the number of metres.

Liquid measures: litres – gallons

litres	*galls or litres*	galls	litres	*galls or litres*	galls
4·6	*1*	0·2	36·4	*8*	1·8
9·1	*2*	0·4	40·9	*9*	2·0
13·6	*3*	0·7	45·5	*10*	2·2
18·2	*4*	0·9	90·9	*20*	4·4
22·7	*5*	1·1	136·4	*30*	6·6

litres	*galls or litres*	galls	litres	*galls or litres*	galls
27·3	*6*	1·3	181·8	*40*	8·8
31·8	*7*	1·5	227·3	*50*	11

1 pint = 0·6 litre 1 litre = 1·8 pint

A rough way to convert from galls to litres: divide by 2 and multiply by 9; from litres to galls: divide by 9 and multiply by 2.

Weight: kilogrammes – pounds

kg.	*lb. or kg.*	lb.	kg.	*lb. or kg.*	lb.
0·5	*1*	2·2	3·2	*7*	15·4
0·9	*2*	4·4	3·6	*8*	17·6
1·4	*3*	6·6	4·1	*9*	19·8
1·8	*4*	8·8	4·5	*10*	22·1
2·3	*5*	11·0	9·1	*20*	44·1
2·7	*6*	13·2	22·7	*50*	110·2

A rough way to convert from lb. to kg.: divide by 11 and multiply by 5; from kg. to lb.: divide by 5 and multiply by 11.

grammes – ounces

grammes	oz.	oz.	grammes
100	3·5	2	57·1
250	8·8	4	114·3
500	17·6	8	228·6
1000 (1 kg.)	35	16 (1 lb.)	457·2

Temperature: centigrade – fahrenheit

centigrade °C	fahrenheit °F	centigrade °C	fahrenheit °F
0	32	20	68
5	41	30	86
10	50	40	104

A rough way to convert from °F to °C: deduct 32 and multiply by 5/9; from °C to °F: multiply by 9/5 and add 32.

VOCABULARY

A		
a, an	un/une	e^{n}/u^{e}n
able (to be)	pouvoir	poo-vwar
about	autour (de)	oh-toor (de^{r})
above	au-dessus (de)	oh de^{r}-su^{e} (de^{r})
abroad	à l'étranger	alay-tra^{n}-zhay
abscess	l'abcès *m*	lab-se
accept (to)	accepter	ak-sep-tay
accident	l'accident *m*	lak-see-dah^{n}
ache	le mal/la douleur	mal/dool-œr
acquaintance	la connaissance	ko-ne-sah^{n}s
across	à travers	a travair
act (to)	jouer	zhoo-ay
actor	l'acteur *m*	lak-tœr
actress	l'actrice *f*	lak-trees
add (to)	ajouter	azhoo-tay
address	l'adresse *f*	la-dres
aeroplane	l'avion *m*	lav-yoh^{n}
afford (to)	avoir les moyens (de)	avwar lay mwa-yah^{n} (de^{r})
afraid	pris de peur	pree de^{r} pœr
after	après	a-pre
afternoon	l'après-midi *m* or *f*	lapre-meedee
again	encore	ah^{n}-kor

against	contre	koh^{n}tr
age	l'âge *m*	lazh
agency	l'agence *f*	la-zhah^{n}s
agent	l'agent *m*	la-zhah^{n}
ago	il y a	eel-ya
agree (to)	consentir	koh^{n}-sah^{n}-teer
ahead	en avant	on-avah^{n}
air	l'air *m*	lair
airbed	le matelas pneumatique	mate^{r}-lah pne^{r}-mat-eek
air-conditioning	la climatisation	klee-mat-eez-asyoh^{n}
airline	la compagnie aérienne	koh^{n}-pan-yee a-ay-ray-en
airmail	par avion	par avyoh^{n}
airport	l'aéroport *m*	la-ay-ro-por
air terminal	l'aérogare *f*	la-ay-ro-gar
alike	semblable	sah^{n}-blabl
all	tout/tous	too/too
allergy	l'allergie *f*	lal-air-zhee
allow (to)	permettre	pair-mettr
all right	bien	bee-a^{n}
almost	presque	preske^{r}
alone	seul	sœl
along	le long de	le^{r} loh^{n} de^{r}

already	déjà	day-zha
alter (to)	changer	shah^{n}-zhay
although	quoique	kwa-ke^{r}
always	toujours	too-zhoor
ambulance	l'ambulance *f*	lah^{n}-bu^{e}lah^{n}s
America	l'Amérique *f*	lamay-reek
American	américain/américaine	amay-reek-ah^{n}(-en)
amuse (to)	amuser	amu^{e}-zay
amusing	amusant	amu^{e}-zah^{n}
anaesthetic	l'anesthésique *m*	lanes-tay-zeek
ancient	ancien	ah^{n}-syah^{n}
and	et	ay
angry	fâché	fash-ay
animal	l'animal *m*	la-nee-mal
ankle	la cheville	she^{r}-vee-y
annoyed	contrarié	koh^{n}-trar-yay
another	un autre/une autre	e^{n} ohtr/u^{e}n ohtr
answer	la réponse	ray-poh^{n}s
answer (to)	répondre	ray-poh^{n}dr
antiques	les antiquités *f*	ah^{n}-tee-kee-tay
antique shop	le magasin d'antiquités	ma-ga-za^{n} dah^{n}-tee-kee-tay
any	aucun	oh-ke^{n}

anyone	quelqu'un	kel-ke^{n}
anything	quelque chose	kel-ke^{r}-shoz
anywhere	quelquepart	kel-ke^{r}-par
apartment	l'appartement *m*	lapar-te^{r}-mah^{n}
apologize (to)	s'excuser	sek-sku^{e}-zay
appendicitis	l'appendicite *f*	la-pah^{n}-dee-seet
appetite	l'appétit *m*	la-pay-tee
apple	la pomme	pom
appointment	le rendez-vous	rah^{n}-day-voo
apricot	l'abricot *m*	lab-ree-koh
April	avril	a-vreel
architect	l'architecte *m*	lar-shee-tekt
architecture	l'architecture *f*	lar-shee-tekt-u^{e}r
arm	le bras	bra
armchair	le fauteuil	foh-tœ-y
army	l'armée *f*	lar-may
around	autour (de)	oh-toor de^{r}
arrange (to)	arranger	arah^{n}-zhay
arrival	l'arrivée *f*	laree-vay
arrive (to)	arriver	aree-vay
art	l'art *m*	lar
art gallery	la galerie d'art	gal-ay-ree-dar
artist	l'artiste *m, f*	lar-teest

as	comme	kom
as much as	autant que	ohtah^{n} ke^{r}
as soon as	aussitôt que	ohsee-toh ke^{r}
as well/also	aussi	ohsee
ashtray	le cendrier	sah^{n}-dree-ay
ask (to)	demander	de^{r}-mah^{n}-day
asleep	endormi	ah^{n}-dor-mee
aspirin	l'aspirine *f*	las-peer-een
at	à	a
at last	enfin	ah^{n}-fa^{n}
at once	immédiatement	ee-may-dee-atmah^{n}
Atlantic	l'Atlantique *m*	lat-lah^{n}-teek
atmosphere	l'atmosphère *f*	lat-mos-fair
attention	l'attention *f*	la-tah^{n}-syoh^{n}
audience	le public	pu^{e}-bleek
August	août	oo
aunt	la tante	tah^{n}t
Australia	l'Australie *f*	loh-stra-lee
Australian	australien/ australienne	oh-stra-lya^{n} (-lyen)
author	l'auteur *m*	loh-tœr
autumn	l'automne *m* or *f*	loh-tah^{n}
available	disponible	dees-poh-neebl

awake	(r) éveillé	(r) ay-vay-yay
away	absent	ab-sah^{n}

B

baby	le bébé	bay-bay
bachelor	le célibataire	say-leeba-tair
back	en arrière	an-ar-yair
back	le dos	doh
bad	mauvais	moh-ve
bag	le sac	sak
baker's	la boulangerie	boo-lah^{n}-zhe^{r}-ee
balcony	le balcon	bal-koh^{n}
ball *dance*	le bal	bal
ball *sport*	la balle	bal
ballet	le ballet	ba-lay
ballpoint pen	le crayon à bille	kray-oh^{n} a beel
banana	la banane	ba-nan
band	l'orchestre *m*	lor-kestr
bandage	le pansement/la bande	pah^{n}-smah^{n}/bah^{n}d
bank	la banque	bah^{n}k
bar	le bar	bar
barber	le coiffeur	kwa-fœr

barman	le serveur/le barman	ser-vœr/bar-man
basket	le panier	pan-yay
bath	la baignoire	ben-ywar
bathe (to)	se baigner	se^{r} ben-yay
bathing cap	le bonnet (de bain)	bo-nay (de^{r} ba^{n})
bathing costume/ trunks	le maillot (de bain)	ma-yoh (de^{r} ba^{n})
bathroom	la salle de bains	sal de^{r} ba^{n}
battery	la pile/la batterie	peel/bat-ree
bay	la baie	be
be (to)	être	etr
beach	la plage	plazh
beard	la barbe	barb
beautiful	beau/belle	boh/bel
beauty parlour	l'institut de beauté *m*	la^{n}-stee-tu^{e} de^{r} boh-tay
because	parce que	par-ske^{r}
bed	le lit	lee
bedroom	la chambre à coucher	shah^{n}-br a koo-shay
beef	le bœuf	bœf
beer	la bière	byair
before *in time*	avant	avah^{n}
before *in space*	devant	de^{r}vah^{n}
begin (to)	commencer	kom-ah^{n}-say

English	French	Pronunciation
beginning	le commencement	kom-ah^{n}-smah^{n}
behind	derrière	der-yer
beige	beige	bezh
Belgian	belge	belzh
Belgium	la Belgique	bel-zheek
believe (to)	croire	krwar
bell	la sonnette	so-nett
belong (to)	appartenir	apar-te^{r}-neer
below	au-dessous (de)	oh-de^{r}-soo (de^{r})
belt	la ceinture	sa^{n}-tu^{e}r
berth	la couchette	koo-shet
best	le meilleur/la meilleure	may-œr
better	mieux/meilleur	myœ/may-œr
between	entre	ah^{n}tr
bicycle	la bicyclette/le vélo	bee-see-klet/ve-loh
big	grand	grah^{n}
bill	la note/l'addition *f*	not/la-dee-syoh^{n}
bird	l'oiseau *m*	lwa-zoh
birthday	l'anniversaire *m*	la-nee-vair-sair
bit	le morceau	mor-soh
bite (to) *insect*	piquer	pee-kay
bite (to) *animal*	mordre	mor-dr

black	noir	nwar
blanket	la couverture	koo-vair-tu^{e}r
bleach (to)	décolorer	day-ko-lor-ay
bleed (to)	saigner	sen-yay
blister	l'ampoule *f*	lah^{n}-pool
blood	le sang	sah^{n}
blouse	le chemisier	she^{r}-mee-zyay
blue	bleu	ble^{r}
boarding house	la pension	pah^{n}-syoh^{n}
boat	le bateau/la barque	bat-oh/bark
body	le corps	kor
boil	le furoncle	fu^{e}-roh^{n}kl
bolster	le traversin	tra-vair-sa^{n}
bolt	le verrou	ve-roo
bone	l'os *m*	los
book	le livre	leevr
book (to)	réserver/louer	ray-sair-vay/loo-ay
booking office	le guichet de location	ghee-shay de^{r} lo-ka-syoh^{n}
bookshop[1]	la librairie	lee-brair-ee
border	la frontière	froh^{n}-tyair
borrow (to)	emprunter	ah^{n}-pre^{n}-tay

1. Old and secondhand bookseller – le bouquiniste, boo-kee-neest.

both	tous les deux	too lay de^{r}
bottle	la bouteille	boo-te-y
bottle opener	l'ouvre-bouteille *m*	loovr-boo-te-y
bottom	le fonds	foh^{n}
bowl	le bol	bol
box *container*	la boîte	bwat
box *theatre*	la loge	lozh
box (to)	boxer	boks-ay
box office	le bureau de location	bu^{e}-roh de^{r} lo-ka-syoh^{n}
boy	le garçon	gar-soh^{n}
bracelet	le bracelet	bra-slay
braces	les bretelles *f*	bre^{r}-tel
brain	le cerveau	sair-voh
brains	la cervelle	sair-vel
brandy	le cognac	kon-yak
brassière	le soutien-gorge	soo-tya^{n} gorzh
bread	le pain	pa^{n}
break (to)	casser	ka-say
breakfast	le petit déjeuner	pe^{r}-tee day-zhe^{r}-nay
breathe (to)	respirer	res-peer-ay
bridge	le pont	poh^{n}
bright	brillant	bree-yah^{n}
bring (to)	apporter	apor-tay

British	britannique	bree-tan-eek
broken	cassé	kas-ay
brooch	la broche	brosh
brother	le frère	frair
brown	brun/marron	bre^{n}/ma-roh^{n}
bruise	le bleu/la contusion	ble^{r}/koh^{n}-tu^{e}-zyoh^{n}
bruise (to)	contusionner	koh^{n}-tu^{e}-zyo-nay
brush	la brosse	bros
brush (to)	brosser	bro-say
bucket	le seau	soh
build (to)	construire	kon-strweer
building	le bâtiment	ba-tee-mah^{n}
bullfight	la course de taureaux	koors de^{r} tor-oh
bullring	l'arène *f*	lar-en
buoy	la bouée	boo-ay
burn	la brûlure	bru^{e}-lu^{e}r
burn (to)	brûler	bru^{e}-lay
burst (to)	éclater/crever	ay-kla-tay/kre^{r}-vay
bus	l'autobus *m*	loh-toh-bu^{e}s
bus stop	l'arrêt *m*	la-re
business	l'affaire *f*	la-fair
busy	occupé	ok-u^{e}-pay
but	mais	me

butcher's	la boucherie	boo-she^{r}-ee
butter	le beurre	bœr
button	le bouton	boo-toh^{n}
buy (to)	acheter	ash-tay
by *near*	près (de)	pre (de^{r})
by *via, means*	par	par

C

cabin	la cabine	ka-been
café	le café	ka-fay
cake	le gâteau	ga-toh
call (to) *summon, name*	appeler	ap-lay
call	l'appel *m*	la-pel
call (to) *telephone*	téléphoner	tay-lay-fo-nay
call *visit*	la visite	vee-zeet
call on, at (to)	rendre visite à	rah^{n}dr vee-zeet a
camera	l'appareil photographique *m*	la-pa-re-y fo-to-gra-feek
camp	le camp	kah^{n}
camp (to)	camper	kah^{n}-pay
camp site	le terrain de camping	te-ra^{n} de^{r} kah^{n}-ping
can (to be able)	pouvoir	poo-vwar
can *tin*	la boîte	bwat
Canada	le Canada	ka-na-da

Canadian	canadien/canadienne	ka-na-dya^{n} (-dyen)
cancel (to)	annuler	anu^{e}-lay
canoe	le canoë	ka-noh-ay
cap	la casquette	kas-ket
capital city	la capitale	ka-pee-tal
car	l'auto *f*/la voiture	loh-toh/vwa-tu^{e}r
car licence *logbook*	la carte grise	kart greez
car park	le parking	par-king
	le parc de stationnement	park de^{r} sta-syon-mah^{n}
carafe	la carafe	karaf
caravan	la caravane	karavan
card	la carte	kart
care	le soin	swa^{n}
careful	soigneux	swan-ye^{r}
carry (to)	porter	por-tay
cash (to)	encaisser	ah^{n}-kes-ay
cashier	le caissier/la caissière	kes-yay (-yair)
casino	le casino	ka-zee-noh
castle	le château	sha-toh
cat	le chat	sha
catalogue	le catalogue	ka-ta-log
catch (to)	attraper	atrap-ay
cathedral	la cathédrale	ka-tay-dral

catholic	catholique	ka-toh-leek
cave	la caverne/la grotte	ka-vairn/grot
centre	le centre	sah^{n}tr
century	le siècle	sy-ekl
ceremony	la cérémonie	say-ray-mon-ee
chair	la chaise	shez
chambermaid	la femme de chambre	fam de^{r} shah^{n}-br
champagne	le champagne	shah^{n}-pan-y
(small) change	la monnaie	mo-nay
change (to)	changer	shah^{n}-zhay
charge	le prix	pree
charge (to)	demander (un prix)	de^{r}-mah^{n}-day (un pree)
cheap	bon marché	bon mar-shay
check (to)	vérifier	vay-reef-yay
cheek	la joue	zhoo
cheese	le fromage	fro-mazh
chemist's	la pharmacie	far-ma-see
cheque	le chèque	shek
cherry	la cerise	ser-eez
chest	la poitrine	pwa-treen
chicken	le poulet	poo-lay
child	l'enfant *m* or *f*	lah^{n}-fah^{n}
chill	le refroidissement	re-frwa-dees-mah^{n}

chin	le menton	mah^{n}-toh^{n}
china	la porcelaine	pors-len
chiropodist	le pédicure	pay-dee-ku^{e}r
chocolate	le chocolat	sho-ko-la
chop	la côtelette	kot-let
Christmas	le Noël	noh-el
church	l'église *f*	lay-gleez
cider	le cidre	seedr
cigar	le cigare	see-gar
cigarette	la cigarette	see-gar-et
cigarette case	l'étui à cigarettes *m*	lay-twee a see-gar-et
cigarette lighter	le briquet	bree-kay
cinema	le cinéma	see-nay-ma
circle *theatre*	la balcon	bal-koh^{n}
circus	le cirque	seerk
city	la grande ville	grah^{n}d veel
class	la classe	klas
clean (to)	nettoyer	ne-tway-ay
clean	propre	propr
cliff	la falaise	fa-lez
cloakroom	le vestiaire	ves-tyair
clock	la pendule/l'horloge *f*	pah^{n}-du^{e}l/lor-lozh
close (to)	fermer	fair-may

closed	fermé	fair-may
cloth	l'étoffe *f*	lay-tof
clothes	les vêtements *m*	vet-mah^{n}
club	le club	klub
coach	l'autocar *m*	loh-toh-kar
coast	la côte	koht
coat	le manteau	mah^{n}-toh
coffee	le café	ka-fay
coin	la pièce de monnaie	pyes de^{r} mo-nay
cold	froid	frwa
cold *med*	le rhume	ru^{e}m
cold cream	le cold-cream	kold-kreem
collar	le col	kol
collar stud	le bouton de col	boo-toh^{n} de^{r} kol
colour	la couleur	koo-lœr
colour film	le film en couleurs	feelm ah^{n} koo-lœr
colour rinse	le rinçage	ra^{n}-sazh
comb	le peigne	pen-y
come (to)	venir	ve^{r}-neer
come in!	entrez!	ah^{n}-tray
comfortable	confortable	koh^{n}-for-tabl
compartment	le compartiment	koh^{n}-par-tee-mah^{n}
complain (to)	se plaindre (de)	se^{r} pla^{n}dr (de^{r})

completely	complètement	koh^{n}-plet-mah^{n}
concert	le concert	koh^{n}-sair
conductor *bus*	le receveur	re^{r}-se^{r}-vœr
conductor *orchestra*	le chef d'orchestre	shef dor-kestr
congratulations!	félicitations!	fay-lee-see-ta-syoh^{n}
constipation	la constipation	koh^{n}-stee-pa-syoh^{n}
consul	le consul	koh^{n}-su^{e}l
consulate	le consulat	koh^{n}-su^{e}-la
contain (to)	contenir	koh^{n}-te^{r}-neer
convenient	commode	ko-mod
convent	le couvent	koo-vah^{n}
conversation	la conversation	koh^{n}-vair-sa-syoh^{n}
cook	le cuisinier/la cuisinière	kwee-zee-nyay (-nyair)
cook (to)	cuire	kweer
cool	frais	fre
copper	le cuivre	kweevr
cork	le bouchon	boo-shoh^{n}
corkscrew	le tire-bouchon	teer boo-shoh^{n}
corner	le coin	kwa^{n}
correct	exact	egza
corridor	le couloir	kool-war
cosmetics	les produits de beauté *m*	pro-dwee de^{r} boh-tay

cost	le prix	pree
cost (to)	coûter	koo-tay
cotton	le coton	ko-toh^{n}
cotton wool	le coton hydrophile	ko-toh^{n} eedro-feel
couchette	la couchette	koo-shet
cough	la toux	too
count (to)	compter	koh^{n}-tay
country *nation*	le pays	pay-ee
country *not town*	la campagne	kah^{n}-pan-y
course *dish*	le plat	pla
cousin	le cousin/la cousine	koo-za^{n} (-zeen)
cramp	la crampe	krah^{n}p
cream	la crème	krem
cross	la croix	krwa
cross (to)	traverser	tra-vair-say
crossroads	le croisement	krwaz-mah^{n}
cufflinks	les boutons de manchette	boo-toh^{n} de^{r} mah^{n}-shet
cup	la tasse	tas
cupboard	l'armoire *f*	lar-mwar
cure (to)	guérir	gay-reer
curl	la boucle	bookl
current	le courant	koo-rah^{n}

curtain	le rideau	ree-doh
customs	la douane	dwa^{n}
customs officer	le douanier	dwan-yay
cut	la coupure	koo-pu^{e}r
cut (to)	couper	koo-pay

D

daily	tous les jours	too lay zhoor
damaged	endommagé	ah^{n}-dom-azh-ay
damp	humide	u^{e}m-eed
dance	la danse/le bal	dah^{n}s/bal
dance (to)	danser	dah^{n}-say
danger	le danger	dah^{n}-zhay
dangerous	dangereux	dah^{n}-zhe^{r}-re^{r}
dark	noir/obscur	nwar/op-sku^{e}r
dark *colour*	foncé	foh^{n}-say
date *time*	la date	dat
daughter	la fille	fee-y
day	le jour/la journée	zhoor/zhoor-nay
dead	mort	mor
deaf	sourd	soor
dear	cher	shair
December	décembre	day-sah^{n}br
decide (to)	décider	day-see-day

deck	le pont	poh^{n}
deckchair	la chaise longue	shez long
declare (to)	déclarer	day-klar-ay
deep	profond	pro-foh^{n}
delay	le retard	re^{r}-tar
delicatessen	la charcuterie	shar-ku^{e}-te^{r}-ree
deliver (to)	distribuer	dee-stree-bu^{e}-ay
demi-pension	la demi-pension	de^{r}-mee pah^{n}-syoh^{n}
dentist	le dentiste	dah^{n}-teest
deodorant	le désodorisant	day-zo-dor-ee-zah^{n}
depart (to)	partir	par-teer
department	le département	day-par-te^{r}-mah^{n}
department store	le grand magasin	grah^{n} ma-ga-za^{n}
departure	le départ	day-par
dessert	le dessert	de-ser
detour	le détour	day-toor
develop *film*	développer	day-vlop-ay
diabetic	diabétique	dya-bay-teek
diamond	le diamant	dya-mah^{n}
diarrhoea	la diarrhée	dya-ray
dictionary	le dictionnaire	deek-syon-air
diet	le régime	ray-zheem
diet (to)	être au régime	etr oh ray-zheem

different	différent	dee-fay-rah^n
difficult	difficile	dee-fee-seel
dine (to)	dîner	dee-nay
dining room	la salle à manger	sal a mah^n-zhay
dinner	le dîner	dee-nay
direction	la direction	dee-rek-syoh^n
dirty	sale	sal
discothèque	la discothèque	dees-koh-tek
dish	le plat	pla
disinfectant	le désinfectant	day-za^n-fek-tah^n
distance	la distance	dee-stah^{n}s
disturb (to)	déranger	day-rah^n-zhay
ditch	le fossé	fo-say
dive (to)	plonger	ploh^n-zhay
diving board	le plongeoir	ploh^n-zhwar
divorced	divorcé(e)	dee-vor-say
dizzy (to feel)	avoir des vertiges *m*	avwar day vair-teezh
do (to)	faire	fair
dock (to)	accoster	akost-ay
doctor	le médecin	mayd-sa^n
dog	le chien	shya^n
doll	la poupée	poo-pay
dollar	le dollar	dolar

door *room*	la porte	port
door *car, train*	la portière	por-tyair
double	double	doobl
double bed	le grand lit	grah^{n} lee
double room	la chambre pour deux	shah^{n}br poor de^{r}
down(stairs)	en bas	ah^{n} ba
dozen	la douzaine	doo-zen
drawer	le tiroir	teer-war
dress	la robe	rob
dressmaker	le couturier/la couturière	koo-tu^{e}r-yay (-yair)
drink (to)	boire	bwar
drinking water	l'eau potable *f*	loh pot-abl
drive (to)	conduire	koh^{n}-dweer
driver	le chauffeur	shoh-fœr
driving licence	le permis de conduire	pair-mee de^{r} koh^{n}-dweer
dry	sec	sek
dry cleaning	le nettoyage à sec	ne-twa-yazh a sek
duck	le canard	ka-nar
during	pendant	pah^{n}-dah^{n}

E

each	chaque	shak

ear	l'oreille *f*	lor-ay
earache	le mal à l'oreille	mal a lor-ay
early	tôt/de bonne heure	toh/de^{r} bon œr
earrings	les boucles d'oreilles *f*	bookl dor-ay
east	l'est *m*	lest
Easter	Pâques	pak
easy	facile	fa-seel
eat (to)	manger	mah^{n}-zhay
egg	l'œuf *m*	lœf
eiderdown	l'édredon *m*	lay-dre^{r}-doh^{n}
elastic	l'élastique *m*	lay-las-teek
elbow	le coude	kood
electric light bulb	l'ampoule *f*	lah^{n}-pool
electric point	la prise de courant	preez de^{r} koo-rah^{n}
elevator	l'ascenseur *m*	la-sah^{n}-sœr
embassy	l'ambassade *f*	lah^{n}-ba-sad
emergency exit	la sortie de secours	sor-tee de^{r} se^{r}-koor
empty	vide	veed
end	la fin	fa^{n}
engaged	fiancé(e)	fyah^{n}-say
England	l'Angleterre *f*	lah^{n}-gle^{r}-tair
English	anglais/anglaise	ah^{n}-gle (-glez)
enjoy (to)	aimer	e-may

enlargement	l'agrandissement *m*	la-grah^{n}-dees-mah^{n}
enough	assez	asay
enquiries	les renseignements *m*	rah^{n}-sen-ye^{r}-mah^{n}
entrance	l'entrée *f*	lah^{n}-tray
envelope	l'enveloppe *f*	lah^{n}-vlop
equipment	l'équipement *m*	lay-keep-mah^{n}
Europe	l'Europe *f*	lœr-op
evening	le soir/la soirée	swar/swar-ay
every	chaque	shak
everybody	tout le monde	too le^{r} moh^{n}d
everything	tout	too
everywhere	partout	par-too
example	l'exemple *m*	leg-zah^{n}pl
excellent	excellent	ek-se-lah^{n}
except	sauf/excepté	sohf/ek-sep-tay
excess	l'excédent *m*	lek-say-dah^{n}
exchange bureau	le bureau de change	bu^{e}-roh der shanzh
excursion	l'excursion *f*	lek-sku^{e}r-zyoh^{n}
exhibition	l'exposition *f*	lek-spo-zee-syoh^{n}
exit	la sortie	sor-tee
expect (to)	attendre	at-ah^{n}dr
expensive	cher	shair
express	exprès	ek-spre

express train	l'express *m*	lek-spres
eye	l'œil *m* (*pl* les yeux)	lœ-y/layz-yœ

F

face	la figure	fee-gu^{e}r
facecream	la crème de beauté	krem de^{r} boh-tay
face powder	la poudre de riz	poodr de^{r} ree
factory	la fabrique/l'usine *f*	fab-reek/lu^{e}-zeen
faint (to)	s'évanouir	say-van-weer
fair	blond	bloh^{n}
fall (to)	tomber	toh^{n}-bay
false teeth	le dentier	dah^{n}-tyay
family	la famille	fa-mee
far	loin	lwa^{n}
fare	le prix du billet	pree du^{e} bee-yay
farm	la ferme	fairm
farther	plus loin	plu^{e} lwa^{n}
fashion	la mode	mod
fast	vite	veet
fat	gras	gra
father	le père	pair
fault	le défaut	day-foh
February	février	fay-vryay

feel (to)	sentir	sah^n-teer
ferry	le ferry	fe-ree
fetch (to)	apporter	a-por-tay
fever	la fièvre	fyevr
few	peu	pœ
fiancé(e)	le fiancé/la fiancée	fyah^n-say
field	le champ	shah^n
fig	la figue	feeg
fill (to)	remplir	rah^n-pleer
filling *tooth*	le plombage	ploh^n-bazh
	l'obturation *f*	lob-tu^e-ra-syoh^n
film	le film	feelm
find (to)	trouver	troo-vay
fine	beau	boh
finger	le doigt	dwa
finish (to)	finir	fee-neer
finished	fini	fee-nee
fire	le feu	fœ
first	premier	pre^{r}m-yay
first class	la première classe	pre^{r}m-yair klas
fish	le poisson	pwa-soh^n
fish (to)	pêcher	pe-shay
fisherman	le pêcheur	pe-shœr

fishing tackle	les articles de pêche *m*	lay zar-teekl de^{r} pesh
fishmonger's	la poissonnerie	pwa-son-e^{r}-ree
flag	le drapeau	dra-poh
flat	plat	pla
flat	l'appartement *m*	la-par-te^{r}-mah^{n}
flight	le vol	vol
flint *lighter*	la pierre	pyair
flippers	les palmes *f*	palm
flood	l'inondation *f*	lee-noh^{n}-da-syoh^{n}
floor *storey*	l'étage *m*	lay-tazh
floor show	le spectacle	spek-takl
florist	le fleuriste	flœr-eest
flower	la fleur	flœr
fly	la mouche	moosh
fog	le brouillard	brwee-yar
follow (to)	suivre	sweevr
food	la nourriture	noo-ree-tu^{e}r
food poisoning	l'intoxication alimentaire *f*	la^{n}-toks-ee-ka-syoh^{n} al-ee-mah^{n}-tair
foot	le pied	pyay
footpath	le sentier	sah^{n}-tyay
for	pour	poor
forehead	le front	froh^{n}

forest	la forêt	for-ay
forget (to)	oublier	oob-ly-ay
fork	la fourchette	foor-shet
forward	en avant	on avah^{n}
forward (to)	faire suivre	fair sweevr
fracture	la fracture	frak-tu^{e}r
fragile	fragile	fra-zheel
France	la France	frah^{n}s
free	libre	leebr
French	français/française	frah^{n}-say (-sez)
fresh	frais	fre
fresh water	l'eau douce *f*	loh doos
Friday	vendredi	vah^{n}-dre^{r}-dee
friend	l'ami *m*/l'amie *f*	la-mee
from	de	de^{r}
front	le devant	de^{r}vah^{n}
fruit	le fruit	frwee
fruiterer	le marchand de fruits	mar-shah^{n} de^{r} frwee
fruit juice	le jus de fruit	zhu^{e} de^{r} frwee
full	plein	pla^{n}
full board	la pension complète	pah^{n}-syoh^{n} kom-plet
funny	drôle	drohl
fur	la fourrure	foo-ru^{e}r

further	plus loin	plu^{e} lwa^{n}
G		
gallery	la galerie	gal-ree
gamble (to)	jouer (de l'argent)	zhoo-ay (de^{r} lar-zhah^{n})
game	la partie	par-tee
garage	le garage	ga-razh
garden	le jardin	zhar-da^{n}
gate	la porte/le portail	port/por-ta-y
gentleman	monsieur	me^{r}-sye^{r}
gentlemen	les toilettes (messieurs)	twa-let (mes-ye^{r})
German	allemand/allemande	al-mah^{n} (-mah^{n}d)
Germany	l'Allemagne *f*	lal-man-y
get (to)	obtenir	ob-te^{r}-neer
get off (to)	descendre	de-sah^{n}dr
get on (to)	monter	moh^{n}-tay
gift	le cadeau	ka-doh
girdle	la gaine	ghen
girl	la jeune fille	zhœn fee-y
give (to)	donner	don-ay
glad	heureux	œr-e^{r}
glass	le verre	vair
glasses	les lunettes *f*	lu^{e}-nett

glove	le gant	gah^{n}
go (to)	aller	alay
goal	le but	bu^{e}
god	Dieu	dye^{r}
gold	l'or *m*	lor
good	bon	boh^{n}
good afternoon	bonjour	boh^{n}-zhoor
good-bye	au revoir	oh re^{r}-vwar
good day/morning	bonjour	boh^{n}-zhoor
good night	bonsoir	boh^{n}-swar
government	le gouvernement	goo-vair-ne^{r}-mah^{n}
granddaughter	la petite-fille	pe^{r}-teet fee-y
grandfather	le grand-père	grah^{n} pair
grandmother	la grand-mère	grah^{n} mair
grandson	le petit-fils	pe^{r}-tee fees
grape	le raisin	re-za^{n}
grapefruit	le/la pamplemousse	pah^{n}-ple^{r}-moos
grass	l'herbe *f*	lerb
grateful	reconnaissant	re^{r}-ko-ne-sah^{n}
gravy	la sauce	sohs
great	grand	grah^{n}
green	vert	vair

greengrocer	le marchand de légumes	mar-shah^{n} de^{r} lay-gu^{e}m
grey	gris	gree
grocer	l'épicier *m*	lay-pee-syay
guarantee	la garantie	gar-ah^{n}-tee
guest	l'invité	la^{n}-vee-tay
guide *book, person*	le guide	gheed
gum	la gencive	zhah^{n}-seev

H

hair	les cheveux *m*	she^{r}-ve^{r}
hair brush	la brosse à cheveux	bros a she^{r}-ve^{r}
haircut	la coupe	koop
hairdresser	le coiffeur	kwa-fœr
hairgrip	la barrette	ba-ret
hairpin	l'épingle	lay-pa^{n}gl
hairset	la mise en plis	meez ah^{n} plee
half	demi	de^{r}-mee
half-board	la demi-pension	de^{r}-mee pah^{n}-syoh^{n}
half fare	une place à demi-tarif	plas a de^{r}-mee ta-reef
ham	le jambon	zhah^{n}-boh^{n}
hand	la main	ma^{n}

handbag	le sac à main	sak a ma^{n}
handkerchief	le mouchoir	moo-shwar
hanger	le cintre	sa^{n}tr
happen (to)	arriver	ar-ee-vay
happy	heureux	œr-e^{r}
happy birthday	bon anniversaire	bon an-ee-vair-sair
Happy Christmas	joyeux Noël	zhway-e^{r} no-el
harbour	le port	por
hard	dur/difficile	du^{e}r/dee-fee-seel
hare	le lièvre	ly-evr
hat	le chapeau	sha-poh
have (to)	avoir	avwar
hay-fever	le rhume des foins	ru^{e}m day fwa^{n}
he	il	eel
head	la tête	tet
headache	le mal de tête	mal de tet
headlight	le phare	far
headwaiter	le maître d'hôtel	metr doh-tel
health	la santé	sah^{n}-tay
hear (to)	entendre	ah^{n}-tah^{n}-dr
heart	le cœur	kœr
heat	la chaleur	sha-lœr
heating	le chauffage	shoh-fazh

heavy	lourd	loor
heel *foot, shoe*	le talon	tal-oh^{n}
hello *telephone*	allô	a-loh
help	l'aide *f*	led
help (to)	aider	ed-ay
hem	l'ourlet *m*	loor-lay
her/his	son *m*/sa *f*/ses *pl*	soh^{n}/sa/say
here	ici	ee-see
hers/his	le sien/la sienne	sya^{n}/syen
high	haut	oh
hike (to)	faire une excursion (à pied)	fair u^{e}n ek-scu^{e}r-zy-oh^{n} a py-ay
hill	la colline	kol-een
him	lui	lwee
hip	la hanche	ah^{n}sh
hire (to)	louer	loo-ay
his/her	son *m*/sa *f*/ses *pl*	soh^{n}/sa/say
his/hers	le sien/la sienne	sya^{n}/syen
hitch hike (to)	faire de l'auto-stop	fair de loh-toh stop
holidays	les vacances *f*	vak-ah^{n}s
(at) home	chez soi/à la maison	shay swa/a la me-zoh^{n}
honey	le miel	myel
honeymoon	la lune de miel	lu^{e}n de^{r} myel

horse	le cheval	she^{r}-val
horse race	la course de chevaux	koors de she^{r}-voh
horse riding	l'équitation	lay-kee-ta-syoh^{n}
hospital	l'hôpital *m*	lop-ee-tal
host	l'hôte *m*	loht
hot	chaud	shoh
hotel	l'hôtel *m*	loh-tel
hotel keeper	l'hôtelier *m*	loh-tel-yay
hot water bottle	la bouillotte	boo-yot
hour	l'heure *f*	lœr
house	la maison	me-zoh^{n}
how?	comment	ko-mah^{n}
how much/many?	combien	koh^{n}-bya^{n}
hungry (to be)	avoir faim	avwar fa^{n}
hurry (to)	se dépêcher	se dap-pesh-ay
hurt (to)	faire mal	fair mal
husband	le mari	ma-ree

I

I	je	zhe^{r}
ice/ice cream	la glace	glas
if	si	see
ill	malade	ma-lad

illness	la maladie	ma-lad-ee
immediately	immédiatement	ee-may-dyat-mah^{n}
important	important	a^{n}-por-tah^{n}
in	dans	dah^{n}
include (to)	comprendre	koh^{n}-prah^{n}dr
included	compris	koh^{n}-pree
inconvenient	inopportun	een-op-or-te^{n}
incorrect	inexact	een-eg-za
indigestion	l'indigestion *f*	la^{n}-dee-zhest-yoh^{n}
infection	l'infection *f*	la^{n}-fek-syoh^{n}
influenza	la grippe	greep
information	les renseignements *m*	rah^{n}-sen-y-mah^{n}
information bureau	le bureau de renseignements	bu^{e}-roh de^{r} rah^{n}-sen-y-mah^{n}
injection	la piqûre	pee-ku^{e}r
ink	l'encre *f*	lah^{n}kr
inn	l'auberge *f*	loh-bairzh
insect	l'insecte *m*	la^{n}-sekt
insect bite	la piqûre (d'insecte)	pee-ku^{e}r
inside	à l'intérieur	a la^{n}-tay-ryœr
instead (of)	au lieu (de)	oh lye^{r} de^{r}
instructor	l'instructeur *m*	la^{n}-stru^{e}k-tœr
insurance	l'assurance *f*	la-su^{e}r-ah^{n}s

insure (to)	assurer	as-u^{e}r-ay
interesting	intéressant	a^{n}-tay-res-ah^{n}
interpreter	l'interprète *m*	la^{n}-tair-pret
into	dans	dah^{n}
introduce (to)	présenter	pray-zah^{n}-tay
invitation	l'invitation *f*	la^{n}-vee-ta-syoh^{n}
invite (to)	inviter	a^{n}-vee-tay
Ireland	l'Irlande *f*	leer-lah^{n}d
Irish	irlandais/irlandaise	eer-lah^{n}-de (-dez)
iron (to)	repasser	re^{r}-pas-ay
island	l'île *f*	leel
it	il/elle	eel/el
Italian	italien/italienne	ee-ta-lya^{n} (-lyen)
Italy	l'Italie *f*	lee-ta-lee

J

jacket	la veste	vest
jam	la confiture	koh^{n}-fee-tu^{e}r
January	janvier	zhah^{n}-vyay
jar	le pot	poh
jaw	la mâchoire	mash-war
jazz	le jazz	zhaz
jelly fish	la méduse	may-du^{e}z

jewellery	la bijouterie	bee-zhoo-tree
journey	le voyage	vwa-yazh
juice	le jus	zhu^{e}
July	juillet	zhwee-ye
jumper	le pullover	pu^{e}l-ovair
June	juin	zhwa^{n}

K

keep (to)	tenir	te^{r}-neer
key	la clé	klay
kidneys	les reins *m*	ra^{n}
kidneys *meat*	les rognons *m*	ron-yoh^{n}
kind	l'espèce *f*	les-pes
king	le roi	rwa
kitchen	la cuisine	kwee-zeen
knee	le genou	zhe^{r}-noo
knickers/briefs	la culotte/le slip	ku^{e}-lot/sleep
knife	le couteau	koo-toh
know (to)	savoir (*a fact*)/ connaître (*a person*)	sa-vwar/kon-etr

L

label	l'étiquette *f*	lay-tee-ket

lace	la dentelle	dah^n-tel
ladies	les toilettes (dames) *f*	twa-let (dam)
lady	la dame	dam
lake	le lac/le bassin (*ornamental*)	lak ba-sa^n
lamb	l'agneau *m*	lan-yoh
lamp	la lampe	lah^{n}p
landing	le palier	pal-yay
landlord/lady	le/la propriétaire	prop-ree-ay-tair
lane	le chemin	she^r-ma^n
language	la langue	lah^{n}g
large	grand	grah^n
last	dernier	dair-nyay
late	tard/en retard	tar/ah^n re^r-tar
laugh (to)	rire	reer
laundry	la blanchisserie	blah^n-shee-se^r-ree
lavatory	les toilettes *f*	twa-let
lavatory paper	le papier hygiénique	pap-yay ee-zhyay-neek
law	la loi	lwa
laxative	le laxatif	lak-sa-teef
lead (to)	conduire	koh^n-dweer
leak (to)	perdre	pairdr
learn (to)	apprendre	ap-rah^{n}dr

leather	le cuir	kweer
leave (to) *abandon*	quitter	kee-tay
leave (to) *go away*	partir	par-teer
left *opp. right*	gauche	gohsh
left luggage	la consigne	koh^n-seen-y
leg	la jambe	zhah^{n}b
lemon	le citron	see-troh^n
lemonade	la limonade	lee-moh^n-ad
lend (to)	prêter	pre-tay
length	la longueur	loh^n-gœr
less	moins	mwa^n
let (to) *rent*	louer	loo-ay
let (to) *allow*	permettre	pair-metr
letter	la lettre	letr
level crossing	le passage à niveau	pa-sazh a nee-voh
library	la bibliothèque	bee-blyoh-tek
licence (driving)	le permis	pair-mee
life	la vie	vee
lift	l'ascenseur *m*	las-ah^n-sœr
light	clair (*colour*)/léger (*weight*)	klair/lay-zhay
light	la lumière	lu^{e}m-yair
light meter	le posemètre	poz-metr

lighter	le briquet	bree-kay
lighter fuel	le gaz/l'essence	gaz/les-ah^{n}s
lighthouse	le phare	far
like (to)	aimer	emay
linen	le linge	la^{n}zh
lingerie	la lingerie	la^{n}zh-ree
lip	la lèvre	levr
lipstick	le rouge à lèvres	roozh a levr
liqueur	la liqueur	lee-kœr
listen (to)	écouter	ay-koo-tay
little	petit (*size*)/peu (*amount*)	pe^{r}-tee/pe^{r}
live (to)	vivre	veevr
liver	le foie	fwa
loaf	le pain	pa^{n}
local	local	lo-kal
lock	la serrure	ser-u^{e}r
long	long/longue	loh^{n}/loh^{n}g
look (to)	regarder	re^{r}-gar-day
look (to) *seem*	avoir l'air	avwar lair
look for (to)	chercher	shair-shay
lorry	le camion	ka-myoh^{n}
lose (to)	perdre	pairdr

lost property office	les objets trouvés *m*	lay zob-zhay troo-vay
lot	beaucoup	boh-koo
loud	bruyant	brwee-ah^{n}
lovely	beau/belle	boh/bel
low	bas	ba
luggage	les bagages *m*	bag-azh
(piece of) luggage	le colis	ko-lee
lunch	le déjeuner	day-zhe^{r}-nay
lung	le poumon	poo-moh^{n}

M

magazine	la revue/le magazine	re^{r}-vu^{e}/ma-ga-zeen
maid	la domestique	dom-est-eek
mail	le courrier	koor-yay
main street	la rue principale	ru^{e} pra^{n}-see-pal
make (to)	fair	fair
make-up	le maquillage	ma-kee-yazh
man	l'homme *m*	lom
manager	le directeur/le patron	dee-rek-tœr/pat-roh^{n}
manicure	les soins des mains	swa^{n} day ma^{n}
many	beaucoup (de)	boh-koo (de^{r})
map *country*	la carte	kart
map *town*	le plan	plah^{n}
March	mars	mars

market	le marché	mar-shay
market place	la place du marché	plas du^{e} mar-shay
marmalade	la confiture d'oranges	kon-fee-tu^{e}r dor-ah^{n}zh
married	marié	mar-yay
Mass	la messe	mes
massage	le massage	mas-azh
match	l'allumette *f*	lal-u^{e}met
match *sport*	le match	match
material	le tissu	tee-su^{e}
matinée	la matinée	ma-tee-nay
mattress	le matelas	mat-la
May	mai	me
me	moi	mwa
meal	le repas	re^{r}-pa
measurements	les mesures *f*	me^{r}-zu^{e}r
meat	la viande	vee-ah^{n}d
mechanic	le mécanicien	may-kan-ee-sya^{n}
medicine	le médicament	may-dee-ka-mah^{n}
meet (to)	rencontrer	rah^{n}-koh^{n}-tray
melon	le melon	me^{r}-loh^{n}
member	le membre	mah^{n}br
mend (to)	raccommoder	ra-ko-mod-ay
menu	le menu	me^{r}-nu^{e}

message	le message	mes-azh
metal	le métal	may-tal
methylated spirit	l'alcool à brûler *m*	al-kol a bru^{e}-lay
midday	midi	mee-dee
middle	le milieu	meel-yœ
midnight	minuit	meen-wee
mild	doux	doo
milk	le lait	le
mine	le mien/la mienne	mya^{n}/myen
mineral water	l'eau minérale *f*	loh meen-ay-ral
minute	la minute	mee-nu^{e}t
mirror	le miroir	meer-war
Miss	Mademoiselle (Mlle)	mad-mwa-zel
miss (to)	manquer	mah^{n}-kay
mistake	l'erreur *f*	ler-œr
modern	moderne	mod-airn
moment	le moment	mo-mah^{n}
Monday	lundi	le^{n}-dee
money	l'argent *m*	lar-zhah^{n}
money order	le mandat	mah^{n}-da
month	le mois	mwa
more	plus/davantage (de)	plu^{e}/dav-ah^{n}-tazh
morning	le matin/la matinée	ma-ta^{n}/ma-tee-nay

mosquito	le moustique	moo-steek
mother	la mère	mair
motor	le moteur	moh-tœr
motor boat	le canot à moteur	kan-oh a moh-tœr
motor cycle	la motocyclette	moh-toh-see-klet
motor racing	la course automobile	koors oh-toh-moh-beel
motorway	l'autoroute *f*	loh-toh-root
mountain	la montagne	moh^{n}-tan-y
mouth	la bouche	boosh
mouthwash	l'eau dentifrice	loh dah^{n}-tee-frees
move (to)	remuer	re^{r}-mu^{e}-ay
Mr	Monsieur (M.)	me^{r}-sye^{r}
Mrs	Madame (Mme)	ma-dam
much	beaucoup (de)	boh-koo
muscle	le muscle	mu^{e}skl
museum	le musée (*art*)/le muséum (*science*)	mu^{e}-zay/mu^{e}-zay-om
music	la musique	mu^{e}-zeek
must (to have to)	devoir	de^{r}-vwar
mustard	la moutarde	moo-tar
mutton	le mouton	moo-toh^{n}
my	mon *m*/ma *f*/mes *pl*	moh^{n}/ma/may
myself	moi-même	mwa-mem

N

nail *finger*	l'ongle *m*	loh^{n}-gl
nailbrush	la brosse à ongles	bros a oh^{n}-gl
nailfile	la lime à ongles	leem a oh^{n}-gl
nail polish	le vernis à ongles	vair-nee a oh^{n}gl
name	le nom	noh^{n}
napkin	la serviette	sair-vyet
nappy	la couche	koosh
narrow	étroit	ay-trwa
near	près (de)	pre
nearly	presque	presk
necessary	nécessaire	nay-ses-air
neck	le cou	koo
necklace	le collier	kol-yay
need (to)	avoir besoin (de)	avwar be^{r}-zwa^{n}
needle	l'aiguille *f*	leg-weey
nerve	le nerf	nair
never	jamais	zha-me
new *brand new*	neuf/neuve	nœf/nœr
new *fresh, latest*	nouveau/nouvelle	noo-voh/noo-vel
news	les nouvelles *f*	noo-vel
newsagent	le marchand de journaux	mar-shah^{n} de^{r} zhoor-noh

newspaper	le journal	zhoor-nal
New Year's Day	le jour de l'an	zhoor de^{r} la^{n}
next	prochain/suivant	pro-sha^{n}/swee-vah^{n}
nice	gentil	zhah^{n}-tee
night	la nuit	nwee
nightclub	la boîte de nuit	bwat de^{r} nwee
nightdress	la chemise de nuit	she^{r}-meez de^{r} nwee
no	non	noh^{n}
nobody	personne	pair-son
noisy	bruyant	brwee-ah^{n}
none	aucun	oh-ke^{n}
north	le nord	nor
nose	le nez	nay
not	ne . . . pas	ne^{r} . . . pa
note *money*	le billet	bee-yay
notebook	le carnet/le cahier	kar-nay/ka-yay
nothing	rien	ry-a^{n}
notice	l'avis *m*	la-vee
notice (to)	remarquer	re^{r}-mar-kay
novel	le roman	ro-mah^{n}
November	novembre	nov-ah^{n}br
number	le numéro	nu^{e}-may-roh
nurse	l'infirmière *f*	a^{n}-fairm-yair

nut	la noix	nwa
nylon	le nylon	nee-loh^{n}
nylons	les bas nylon *m*	ba nee-loh^{n}

O

occupation	le métier	may-tyay
occupied	occupé	ok-u^{e}pay
ocean	l'océan *m*	lo-say-ah^{n}
October	octobre	okt-obr
odd *strange*	singulier	sa^{n}-gu^{e}-lyay
of	de	de^{r}
office	le bureau	bu^{e}-roh
official	officiel	of-ee-syel
often	souvent	soo-vah^{n}
oil	l'huile *f*	lweel
oily	gras	gra
ointment	la pommade	po-mad
old	vieux/vieille	vye^{r}/vya-y
olive	l'olive *f*	lol-eev
on	sur	su^{e}r
once	une fois	fwa
one way street	la rue à sens unique	ru^{e} a sah^{n}-su^{e}-neek
only *adj/adv*	seul/seulement	sœl/sœl-mah^{n}

open (to)	ouvrir	oo-vreer
open *pp*	ouvert	oo-vair
opera	l'opéra *m*	lop-ay-ra
operation	l'opération *f*	lop-ay-ra-syoh^{n}
opportunity	l'occasion *f*	lo-ka-zyoh^{n}
opposite	en face (de)	ah^{n} fas
optician	l'opticien *m*	lop-tee-sya^{n}
or	ou	oo
orange	orange	orah^{n}zh
orchestra	l'orchestre *m*	lor-kestr
order (to)	commander	ko-mah^{n}-day
ordinary	ordinaire	or-dee-nair
other	autre	ohtr
our	notre *s*/nos *pl*	notr/noh
ours	le/la nôtre	nohtr
out of order	détraqué	day-trak-ay
outside	dehors	de^{r}-or
over	au-dessus (de)	oh-de^{r}-su^{e}
over *finished*	fini	fee-nee
overcoat	le pardessus	par-de^{r}-su^{e}
over there	là-bas	la-ba
owe (to)	devoir	de-vwar
owner	le propriétaire	prop-ree-ay-tair

P

pack (to)	faire la valise	fair la va-leez
packet	le paquet	pa-kay
page	la page	pazh
paid	payé	pay-ay
pain	la douleur	doo-lœr
paint (to)	peindre	pa^{n}dr
painting	la peinture	pa^{n}-tu^{e}r
pair	la paire	pair
palace	le palais/le château	pa-le/sha-toh
pale	pâle/blême	pal/blem
paper	le papier	pap-yay
paraffin	le pétrole	pay-trol
parcel	le colis/le paquet	ko-lee/pa-kay
park (to)	stationner	sta-syon-ay
park	le parc	park
part	la partie	par-tee
parting *hair*	la raie	re
party	la réception	ray-sep-syoh^{n}
pass (to)	passer	pas-ay
passenger	le voyageur (*train*)	vwa-ya-zhœr
	le passager (*sea, air*)	pas-azh-ay
passport	le passeport	pas-por

path	le sentier	sah^{n}-tyay
patient	le/la malade	ma-lad
pavement	le trottoir	trot-war
pay (to)	payer	pay-ay
peach	la pêche	pesh
peak	la cime	seem
pear	la poire	pwar
pearl	la perle	pairl
pebble	le galet	ga-lay
pedal	la pédale	pay-dal
pedestrian	le piéton	pyay-toh^{n}
pen	le stylo	stee-loh
pencil	le crayon	kray-oh^{n}
penknife	le canif	ka-neef
people	les gens *m*	zhah^{n}
pepper *spice*	le poivre	pwavr
perfect	parfait	par-fe
performance	la représentation	re^{r}-pray-sah^{n}-ta-syoh^{n}
perfume	le parfum	pra-fa^{n}
perhaps	peut-être	pe^{r}t-etr
perishable	périssable	pay-ree-sabl
perm	la permanente	pair-ma-nant
permit	le permis	pair-mee

permit (to)	permettre	pair-metr
person	la personne	pair-son
personal	personnel	pair-son-el
petrol	l'essence *f*	les-ah^{n}s
petrol station	le poste d'essence	post des-ah^{n}s
petticoat	la jupe	zhu^{e}p
photograph	la photographie	fo-to-gra-fee
photographer	le photographe	fo-to-graf
piano	le piano	pya-no
picnic	le pique-nique	peek-neek
piece	le morceau	mor-soh
pier	la jetée	zhe^{r}-tay
pill	la pilule	pee-lu^{e}l
pillow	l'oreiller *m*	lor-ay-yay
pin	l'épingle *f*	lay-pa^{n}gl
pineapple	l'ananas *m*	la-na-na
pink	rose	roz
pipe	la pipe	peep
place	l'endroit *m*	lah^{n}-drwa
plain	simple	sa^{n}pl
plan	le plan	plah^{n}
(adhesive) plaster	le sparadrap/le tricostéril	spa-ra-dra/tree-ko-stair-eel

plastic	le plastique	plas-teek
plate	l'assiette *f*	las-yet
platform	le quai	ke
play (to)	jouer	zhoo-ay
play	la pièce (de théâtre)	pyes (de^{r} tay-atr)
please	s'il vous plaît	seel voo ple
plenty	beaucoup (de)	boh-koo
plug	le bouchon	boo-shoh^{n}
plum	la prune	pru^{e}n
pocket	la poche	posh
point	le point	pwa^{n}
poisonous	venimeux (*animal*)	ve-nee-mœ
	vénéneux (*plant*)	vay-nay-nœ
policeman	l'agent de police *m*	la-zhah^{n} de^{r} po-lees
police station	le poste de police	post de^{r} po-lees
poor	pauvre	pohvr
pope	le Pape	pap
popular	populaire	po-pu^{e}-lair
pork	le porc	por
port	le port	por
porter	le porteur	por-tœr
possible	possible	po-seebl
post (to)	mettre à la poste	metr a la post

post box	la boîte aux lettres	bwat oh letr
postcard	la carte postale	kart pos-tal
postman	le facteur	fak-tœr
post office	le bureau de poste	bu^{e}-roh de^{r} post
poste restante	la poste restante	post res-tah^{n}t
potato	la pomme de terre	pom de^{r} tair
pound	la livre	leevr
prefer (to)	préférer	pray-fay-ray
prepare (to)	préparer	pray-par-ay
prescription	l'ordonnance *f*	lor-don-ah^{n}s
present *gift*	le cadeau	ka-doh
press (to)	repasser	re^{r}-pas-ay
pretty	joli	zho-lee
price	le prix	pree
priest	le prêtre	pretr
private	privé	pree-vay
problem	le problème	pro-blem
profession	la profession	pro-fes-yoh^{n}
programme	le programme	pro-gram
promise	la promesse	pro-mes
promise (to)	promettre	pro-metr
protestant	protestant	pro-test-ah^{n}
pull (to)	tirer	tee-ray

pump	la pompe	poh^{n}p
pure	pur	pu^{e}r
purse	le porte-monnaie	port mo-nay
push (to)	pousser	poo-say
put (to)	mettre	metr
pyjamas	le pyjama	pee-zha-ma

Q

quality	la qualité	kal-ee-tay
quantity	la quantité	kah^{n}-tee-tay
quarter	le quart	kar
queen	la reine	ren
question	la question	kes-tyoh^{n}
quick	rapide	ra-peed
quiet	tranquille	trah^{n}-keel
quite	tout à fait	too-ta-fe

R

rabbit	le lapin	la-pa^{n}
racecourse	l'hippodrome *m*	lee-po-drom
races	les courses *f*	koors
radiator	le radiateur	ra-dya-tœr

radio	la radio	ra-dyoh
railway	le chemin de fer	shma^{n} de^{r} fair
rain	la pluie	plwee
rain (to)	pleuvoir	plœ-vwar
raincoat	l'imperméable *m*	la^{n}-pair-may-abl
rangefinder	le télémètre	tay-lay-metr
rare	rare	rar
raspberry	la framboise	frah^{n}-bwaz
rather	plutôt	plu^{e}-toh
raw	cru	cru^{e}
razor	le rasoir	ra-zwar
razor blade	la lame à rasoir	lam a ra-zwar
read (to)	lire	leer
ready	prêt	pre
real	vrai	vre
really	vraiment	vre-mah^{n}
reason	la raison	re-zoh^{n}
receipt	la quittance	kee-tah^{n}s
receive (to)	recevoir	re^{r}-se^{r}-vwar
recent	récent	ray-sah^{n}
recommend (to)	recommander	re^{r}-ko-mah^{n}-day
record *music*	le disque	deesk
red	rouge	roozh

refreshment room	le buffet/la buvette	bu^{e}-fay/bu^{e}-vet
register (to)	enregistrer	ah^{n}-rezh-ees-tray
	recommander (*letter*)	re^{r}-ko-mah^{n}-day
registered mail	le courrier recommandé	koo-ryay re^{r}-ko-mah^{n}-day
religion	la religion	re^{r}-lee-zhyoh^{n}
remember (to)	se souvenir (de)	se^{r} soov-neer
rent	le loyer	lwa-yay
repair (to)	réparer	ray-par-ay
repeat (to)	répéter	ray-pay-tay
reply (to)	répondre	ray-poh^{n}dr
reply paid	la réponse payée	ray-poh^{n}s pay-ay
reservation	la réservation	ray-zair-va-syoh^{n}
reserve (to)	réserver	ray-zair-vay
restaurant	le restaurant	res-tor-ah^{n}
restaurant car	le wagon-restaurant	va-goh^{n} res-tor-ah^{n}
return (to) *come back*	revenir	re^{r}v-neer
return (to) *go back*	retourner	re^{r}-toor-nay
return (to) *give back*	rendre	rah^{n}dr
rib	la côte	koht
ribbon	le ruban	ru^{e}-bah^{n}
right *opp. left*	droit	drwa
ring	la bague	bag

river	le fleuve/la rivière[1]	flœv/reev-yair
road *between towns*	la route	root
road *within towns*	la rue	ru^{e}
rock	le rocher	ro-shay
roll *bread*	le petit pain	pe^{r}-tee pa^{n}
roller *hair*	le rouleau	roo-loh
room	la chambre	shah^{n}br
rope	la corde	kord
round	rond	roh^{n}
rowing boat	le bateau à rames	ba-toh a ram
rubber	caoutchouc	ka-oot-shoo
rubbish	les ordures *f*	lay zor-du^{e}r
rucksack	le sac à dos	sak a doh
rude	grossier	groh-syay
run (to)	courir	koo-reer
Russia	la Russie	ru^{e}-see
Russian	russe	ru^{e}s

S

safe	sauf	sohf
sailor	le marin	ma-ra^{n}

1. 'Fleuve' is used for rivers that flow into the sea and 'rivière' for rivers that flow into other rivers.

salad	la salade	sa-lad
salesgirl	la vendeuse	vah^{n}-dœz
salesman	le vendeur	vah^{n}-dœr
salt	le sel	sel
salt water	l'eau salée *f*	loh sa-lay
same	le/la même	mem
sand	le sable	sabl
sandal	la sandale	sah^{n}-dal
sandwich	le sandwich	sah^{n}d-weech
sanitary towel	la serviette hygiénique	sair-vyet ee-zhyay-neek
satin	le satin	sa-ta^{n}
Saturday	samedi	sam-dee
sauce	la sauce	sohs
saucer	la soucoupe	soo-koop
say (to)	dire	deer
scald oneself (to)	s'ébouillanter	say-bwee-yah^{n}-tay
scarf	le foulard	foo-lar
scent	le parfum	par-fa^{n}
school	l'école *f*	lay-kol
scissors	les ciseaux *m*	see-zoh
Scotland	l'Ecosse *f*	lay-kos
Scottish	écossais/écossaise	ay-ko-se (-sez)

scratch (to)	égratigner	ay-gra-teen-yay
screw	la vis	vees
sculpture	la sculpture	sku^{e}l-tu^{e}r
sea	la mer	mair
seasickness	le mal de mer	mal de^{r} mair
season	la saison	se-zoh^{n}
seat	la place	plas
second	deuxième	de^{r}z-yem
second class	la deuxième classe	de^{r}z-yem klas
sedative	le sédatif	say-da-teef
see (to)	voir	vwar
sell (to)	vendre	vah^{n}-dr
seem (to)	sembler	sah^{n}-blay
send (to)	envoyer	ah^{n}-vwa-yay
separately	séparément	say-pa-ray-mah^{n}
September	septembre	sep-tah^{n}br
serious	sérieux	sayr-ye^{r}
serve (to)	servir	sair-veer
served	servi	sair-vee
service	le service	sair-vees
service *church*	l'office *m*	lo-fees
several	plusieurs	plu^{e}-zyœr
sew (to)	coudre	koodr

shade *colour*	la teinte	ta^{n}t
shade *sun*	l'ombre *f*	loh^{n}br
shallow	peu profond	pœ pro-foh^{n}
shampoo	le shampooing	shah^{n}-pwa^{n}
shape	la forme	form
share (to)	partager	par-ta-zhay
sharp	aigu/pointu	egu^{e}/pwa^{n}-tu^{e}
shave (to)	se raser	se^{r} ra-zay
shaving brush	le blaireau	ble-roh
shaving cream	la crème à raser	krem a ra-zay
she	elle	el
sheet	le drap	dra
shell	le coquillage	ko-kee-yazh
shelter	l'abri *m*	la-bree
shine (to)	briller	bree-yay
shingle	le galet	ga-lay
ship	le bateau	ba-toh
shipping line	la compagnie de navigation	koh^{n}-pan-yee de^{r} na-vee-ga-syoh^{n}
shirt	la chemise	she^{r}-meez
shoe	le soulier/la chaussure	soo-lyay/shoh-su^{e}r
shoelace	le lacet (de soulier)	la-say
shoe shop	le magasin de chaussures	ma-ga-za^{n} de^{r} shoh-su^{e}r

shoe repairs	la cordonnerie	kor-don-ree
shop	le magasin	ma-ga-za^{n}
short	court	koor
shorts	le short	shor
shoulder	l'épaule *f*	lay-pohl
show *theatre*	le spectacle	spek-takl
show (to)	montrer	moh^{n}-tray
shower	la douche	doosh
shut (to)	fermer	fair-may
shut *pp*	fermé	fair-may
shutter	le volet	vo-lay
sick	malade	ma-lad
side	le côté	koh-tay
sights	les monuments *m*	mon-u^{e}-mah^{n}
	les curiosités *f*	ku^{e}-ree-ozee-tay
sightseeing (to go)	visiter les monuments	vee-zee-tay lay mon-u^{e}-mah^{n}
silk	la soie	swa
silver	l'argent *m*	lar-zhah^{n}
simple	simple	sa^{n}pl
since	depuis	de^{r}-pwee
single	seul	sœl
single room	la chambre pour une personne	shah^{n}br poor u^{e}n pair-son

sister	la sœur	sœr
sit down (to)	s'asseoir	sas-war
sitting	assis	asee
size	la grandeur	grah^{n}-dœr
skate (to)	patiner	pa-tee-nay
skating	le patinage	pa-tee-nazh
ski (to)	skier	skee-ay
skid (to)	déraper	day-rap-ay
skiing	le ski	skee
sky	le ciel	sy-el
sleep (to)	dormir	dor-meer
sleeper	le wagon-lit	va-goh^{n} lee
sleeping bag	le sac de couchage	sak de^{r} koo-shazh
sleeve	la manche	mah^{n}sh
slice	la tranche	trah^{n}sh
slip	la combinaison	koh^{n}-bee-ne-zoh^{n}
slipper	la pantoufle	pah^{n}-toofl
slowly	lentement	lah^{n}-te^{r}-mah^{n}
small	petit	pe^{r}-tee
smart	chic	sheek
smell (to)	sentir	sah^{n}-teer
smoke (to)	fumer	fu^{e}-may

smoking compartment	le compartiment fumeur	koh^{n}-par-tee-mah^{n} fu^{e}-mœr
(no) smoking	défense de fumer	day-fah^{n}s de^{r} fu^{e}-may
snack	le repas léger	re^{r}-pa lay-zhay
snow	la neige	nezh
snow (to)	neiger	nezh-ay
so	si	see
soap	le savon	sav-oh^{n}
soap powder	le savon en paillettes	sav-oh^{n} ah^{n} pa-yet
sock	la chaussette	shoh-set
soda	le soda	soda
sold	vendu	vah^{n}-du^{e}
sole *shoe*	la semelle	se^{r}-mel
some	quelque	kel-ke^{r}
somebody	quelqu'un	kel-ke^{n}
something	quelque chose	kel-ke^{r}-shoz
sometimes	quelquefois	kel-ke^{r}-fwa
somewhere	quelque part	kel-ke^{r}-par
son	le fils	fees
song	la chanson	shah^{n}-soh^{n}
soon	bientôt	bya^{n}-toh
sore throat	le mal de gorge	mal de^{r} gorzh
sorry	pardon	par-doh^{n}

sort	l'espèce *f*	les-pes
soup	la soupe	soop
sour	aigre	egr
south	le sud	su^{e}d
souvenir	le souvenir	soov-neer
Spain	l'Espagne *f*	les-pan-y
Spanish	espagnol	es-pan-yol
speak (to)	parler	par-lay
speciality	la spécialité	spay-syal-ee-tay
speed	la vitesse	vee-tes
speed limit	la limitation de vitesse	lee-mee-ta-syoh^{n} de^{r} vee-tes
spend (to)	dépenser (*money*)	day-pah^{n}-say
	passer (*time*)	pa-say
spoon	la cuiller	kwee-yair
sport	le sport	spor
sprain	la foulure	foo-lu^{e}r
sprain (to)	se fouler	se^{r} foo-lay
spring	le printemps	pra^{n}-tah^{n}
square *n*	la place	plas
stage	la scène	sen
stain	la tache	tash
stained	taché	ta-shay

stairs	l'escalier *m*	les-kal-yay
stale	pas frais	pa fre
stalls	les fauteuils d'orchestre *m*	foh-tœ-y dor-kestr
stamp	le timbre	ta^{n}br
stand (to)	se tenir debout	se^{r} te^{r}-neer de^{r}-boo
start (to)	commencer	ko-mah^{n}-say
station	la gare	gar
station *tube*	la station	sta-syoh^{n}
stationer's	la papeterie	pa-pe-tree
statue	la statue	sta-tu^{e}
stay (to)	rester	res-tay
steak	le bifteck	beef-tek
step	le pas	pa
stew	le ragoût	ra-goo
steward	le steward (*airline*)	stew-ar
	le garçon de cabine (*ship*)	gar-soh^{n} de^{r} ka-been
stewardess	la stewardess	stew-ar-des
still	toujours/encore	too-zhoor/ah^{n}-kor
sting	la piqûre	pee-ku^{e}r
stocking	le bas	ba
stolen	volé	vo-lay
stomach	l'estomac *m*	les-to-mak

stomach ache	le mal au ventre	mal-oh-vah^{n}tr
stone	la pierre	py-air
stop (to)	s'arrêter	sa-re-tay
store	le magasin	ma-ga-za^{n}
stove	le réchaud	ray-shoh
straight	droit	drwa
straight on	tout droit	too drwa
strange	étrange	ay-trah^{n}zh
strawberry	la fraise	frez
stream	le ruisseau	rwee-soh
street	la rue	ru^{e}
string	la ficelle	fee-sel
strong	fort	for
student	l'étudiant (-e)	lay-tu^{e}-dyah^{n} (t)
stung (to be)	être piqué	etr pee-kay
style	le style	steel
suburb	la banlieue	ban^{n}-lye^{r}
subway	le passage souterrain	pa-sazh soo-ter-a^{n}
suede	le daim	da^{n}
sugar	le sucre	su^{e}kr
suit	le costume (*men*)	kos-tu^{e}m
	le tailleur (*women*)	ta-yœr
suitcase	la valise	va-leez

summer	l'été *m*	lay-tay
sun	le soleil	so-lay
sunbathe (to)	se bronzer	se^{r} broh^{n}-zay
	prendre un bain de soleil	prah^{n}dr e^{n} ba^{n} de^{r} sol-ay
sunburn	le coup de soleil	koo de^{r} sol-ay
Sunday	dimanche	dee-mah^{n}sh
sunglasses	les lunettes de soleil *f*	lu^{e}-net de^{r} sol-ay
sunhat	le chapeau de paille	sha-poh de^{r} pa-y
sunny	ensoleillé	ah^{n}-sol-ay-yay
sunshade	l'ombrelle *f*	lom-brel
sunstroke	l'insolation *f*	la^{n}-so-la-syoh^{n}
suntan oil	l'huile solaire *f*	lweel sol-air
supper	le souper	soo-pay
supplementary charge	le supplément	su^{e}-play-mah^{n}
sure	sûr	su^{e}r
surface mail	le courrier ordinaire	koor-yay or-dee-nair
surgery	le cabinet	ka-bee-nay
suspender belt	le porte-jarretelles	port zhar-tel
sweater	le sweater	swe-tair
sweet	sucré	su^{e}-kray
sweet	le bonbon	boh^{n}-boh^{n}
swell (to)	enfler	ah^{n}-flay

swim (to)	nager	na-zhay
swimming pool	la piscine	pee-seen
Swiss	suisse	swees
switch *light*	l'interrupteur *m*	la^{n}-tay-ru^{e}p-tœr
Switzerland	la Suisse	swees
swollen	enflé	ah^{n}-flay
synagogue	la synagogue	see-na-gog

T

table	la table	tabl
tablecloth	la nappe	nap
tablet	le comprimé	koh^{n}-pree-may
tailor	le tailleur	ta-yœr
take (to)	prendre	prah^{n}dr
talk (to)	parler	par-lay
tall	grand	grah^{n}
tank	le réservoir	ray-sair-vwar
tap	le robinet	ro-bee-nay
taste	le goût	goo
tax	la taxe	taks
taxi	le taxi	tak-see
taxi rank	la station de taxis	sta-syoh^{n} de^{r} tak-see
tea	le thé	tay

teach (to)	enseigner	ah^{n}-sen-yay
telegram	le télégramme	tay-lay-gram
telephone (to)	téléphoner	tay-lay-fon-ay
telephone	le téléphone	tay-lay-fon
telephone box	la cabine téléphonique	ka-been tay-lay-fon-eek
telephone call	le coup de téléphone	koo de^{r} tay-lay-fon
telephone directory	le bottin	bo-ta^{n}
telephone number	le numéro de téléphone	nu^{e}-may-roh de^{r} tay-lay-fon
telephone operator	le/la standardiste	stah^{n}-dar-deest
telephone token	le jeton (de téléphone)	zhe^{r}-toh^{n}
television	la télévision	tay-lay-vee-zyoh^{n}
tell (to)	dire	deer
temperature	la témperature	tah^{n}-pay-ra-tu^{e}r
temple	le temple	tah^{n}pl
temporary	temporaire	tah^{n}-por-air
tent	la tente	tah^{n}t
tent peg	le piquet (de tente)	pee-kay
tent pole	le montant (de tente)	moh^{n}-tah^{n}
terrace	la terrasse	ter-as
than	que	ke^{r}
thank you	merci	mair-see

that	cela	sla
the	le/la/les	le^{r}, la, lay
theatre	le théâtre	tay-atr
their	leur	lœr
them	leur/eux	lœr/e^{r}
then	alors	alor
there	là	la
there is/are	il y a	eel-ya
thermometer	le thermomètre	tair-mom-etr
these	ces	say
they	ils/elles	eel/el
thick	épais	ay-pe
thin	mince	ma^{n}s
thing	la chose	shohz
think (to)	penser	pah^{n}-say
thirsty (to be)	avoir soif	av-war swaf
this	ce/cet/cette	se^{r}/set/set
though	quoique	kwa-ke^{r}
thread	le fil	feel
throat	la gorge	gorzh
through	à travers/par	a tra-vair/par
throw (to)	lancer/jeter	lah^{n}-say/zhe^{r}-tay
thumb	le pouce	poos

Thursday	jeudi	zhe^r-dee
ticket	le billet	bee-yay
tide	la marée	ma-ray
tie	la cravate	kra-vat
tight	serré	se-ray
time	le temps/l'heure *f*	tah^n/lœr
timetable	l'horaire *m*	lor-air
tin	la boîte	bwat
tin opener	l'ouvre-boîte *m*	loovr bwat
tint (to)	colorer	ko-lor-ay
tip	le pourboire	poor-bwar
tip (to)	donner un pourboire	do-nay e^n poor-bwar
tired (to be)	être fatigué	etr fa-tee-gay
tissues	les mouchoirs en papier	moo-shwar ah^n pap-yay
to	à/pour	a/poor
toast	le pain grillé	pa^n gree-yay
tobacco (brown)	le tabac (brun)	ta-bak (bre^n)
tobacco pouch	la blague à tabac	blag a ta-bak
tobacconist's	le bureau de tabac	bu^e-roh de^r ta-bak
today	aujourd'hui	oh-zhoor-dwee
toe	l'orteil *m*	lor-tay
together	ensemble	ah^n-sah^nbl

toilet	la toilette	twa-let
toilet paper	le papier hygiénique	pap-yay ee-zhyay-neek
tomato	la tomate	to-mat
tomorrow	demain	de^{r}-ma^{n}
tongue	la langue	lah^{n}g
tonight	ce soir	se^{r} swar
tonsils	les amygdales *f*	lay zam-ee-dal
too *also*	aussi	oh-see
too, too much/many	trop (de)	troh
tooth	la dent	dah^{n}
toothache	le mal aux dents	mal oh dah^{n}
toothbrush	la brosse à dents	bros a dah^{n}
toothpaste	la pâte dentifrice	pat dah^{n}-tee-frees
toothpick	le cure-dents *m*	ku^{e}r dah^{n}
top	le sommet	som-me
torch	la lampe (de poche)	lah^{n}p
torn	déchiré	day-sheer-ay
touch (to)	toucher	too-shay
tour	le tour/la visite	toor/vee-zeet
tourist	le touriste	toor-eest
tow (to)	remorquer	re^{r}-mor-kay
towards	vers	vair
towel	la serviette	sair-vyet

tower	la tour	toor
town	la ville	veel
town hall	l'hôtel de ville *m*	lo-tel de^{r} veel
toy	le jouet	zhoo-ay
traffic	la circulation	seer-ku^{e}-la-syoh^{n}
traffic jam	l'embouteillage *m*	lah^{n}-boo-tay-azh
traffic lights	les feux *m*	fe^{r}
trailer	la remorque	re^{r}-mork
train	le train	tra^{n}
translate (to)	traduire	tra-dweer
travel (to)	voyager	vwa-ya-zhay
travel agency	l'agence de voyage *f*	la-zhah^{n}s de^{r} vwa-yazh
traveller	le voyageur	vwa-ya-zhœr
travellers' cheque	le chèque de voyage	shek de^{r} vwa-yazh
treatment	le traitement	tret-mah^{n}
tree	l'arbre *m*	larbr
trim (to) *hair*	rafraîchir	ra-fre-sheer
trip	l'excursion *f*	lek-sku^{e}r-syoh^{n}
trouble	les ennuis *m*	lay-zah^{n}-nwee
trousers	le pantalon	pah^{n}-ta-loh^{n}
true	vrai	vre
trunk *luggage*	la malle	mal
trunks	le caleçon	kal-soh^{n}

try, try on (to)	essayer	esay-yay
Tuesday	mardi	mar-dee
tunnel	le tunnel	tu^{e}-nel
turn (to)	tourner	toor-nay
turning	le tournant	toor-nah^{n}
twisted	tordu	tor-du^{e}

U

ugly	laid	le
umbrella	le parapluie	para-plwee
(beach) umbrella	le parasol	para-sol
uncle	l'oncle *m*	loh^{n}kl
uncomfortable	mal à l'aise	mal al-ez
under	sous	soo
underground	le métro	may-troh
understand	comprendre	koh^{n}-prah^{n}dr
underwater fishing	la pêche sous-marine	pesh soo ma-reen
underwear	les sous-vêtements *m*	soo vet-mah^{n}
university	l'université *f*	lu^{e}-nee-vair-see-tay
unpack (to)	défaire les bagages	day-fair lay bag-azh
until	jusqu'à	zhu^{e}s-ka
unusual	peu commun	pe^{r} kom-e^{n}
up(stairs)	en haut	ah^{n}-oh

urgent	urgent	u^{e}r-zhah^{n}
use (to)	employer	ah^{n}-plwa-yay
	se servir (de)	se^{r} sair-veer de^{r}
usual	habituel/ordinaire	a-bee-tu^{e}-el/or-dee-nair

V

vacancies	chambres libres *f*	shah^{n}br leebr
vacant	libre	leebr
vacation	les vacances *f*	va-kah^{n}s
vaccination	la vaccination	vak-see-na-syoh^{n}
valid	valable	va-labl
valley	la vallée	va-lay
valuable	précieux	pray-sye^{r}
value	la valeur	va-lœr
vase	le vase	vahz
vegetable	le légume	lay-gu^{e}m
vegetarian	le végétarien	vay-zhay-ta-rya^{n}
veil	le voile	vwal
vein	la veine	ven
ventilation	l'aération	la-ay-ra-syoh^{n}
very	très	tre
very much	beaucoup	boh-koo
view	la vue	vu^{e}

village	le village	vee-lazh
vinegar	le vinaigre	vee-negr
violin	le violon	vyo-loh^{n}
visa	le visa	vee-za
visit	la visite	vee-zeet
visit (to)	visiter	vee-zee-tay
voice	la voix	vwa
voltage	le voltage	vol-tazh
vomit (to)	vomir	vo-meer
voyage	le voyage	vwa-yazh

W

wait (to)	attendre	at-ah^{n}dr
waiter	le garçon	gar-soh^{n}
waiting room	la salle d'attente	sal da-tah^{n}t
waitress	la serveuse	sair-vœz
wake (to)	se réveiller	se^{r} ray-vay-ay
Wales	le Pays de Galles	pay-ee de^{r} gal
walk	la promenade	prom-nad
walk (to)	marcher/se promener	mar-shay/se^{r} prom-nay
wallet	le portefeuille	port-fœ-y
want (to)	vouloir/avoir besoin (de)	vool-war/avwar be^{r}-zwa^{n}

wardrobe	l'armoire *f*	lar-mwar
warm	chaud	shoh
wash (to)	laver	la-vay
washbasin	le lavabo	la-va-boh
watch	la montre	moh^{n}tr
water (fresh, salt)	l'eau *f* (douce, salée)	loh (doos, sa-lay)
waterfall	la chute d'eau	shu^{e}t doh
water melon	la pastèque	pas-tek
water ski(-ing)	le ski nautique	skee noh-teek
wave *sea*	la vague	vag
wave *hair*	l'ondulation *f*	oh^{n}-du^{e}-la-syoh^{n}
way	le chemin	shma^{n}
we	nous	noo
wear (to)	porter	por-tay
weather	le temps	tah^{n}
Wednesday	mercredi	mair-kre^{r}-dee
week	la semaine	se^{r}-men
weigh (to)	peser	pe^{r}-say
well	bien	by-a^{n}
Welsh	gallois/galloise	gal-wa (-waz)
west	l'ouest *m*	lwest
wet	mouillé	mwee-yay
what ?	quel/quelle ?	kel

wheel	la roue	roo
when ?	quand ?	kah^{n}
where ?	où ?	oo
which ?	quel(s)/quelle(s) ?	kel
while	pendant que	pah^{n}-dah^{n} ke^{r}
white	blanc	blah^{n}
who ?	qui ?	kee
whole	le tout	too
whose ?	à qui ?	a kee
why ?	pourquoi ?	poor-kwa
wide	large	larzh
widow	la veuve	vœv
widower	le veuf	vœf
wife	la femme	fam
wild	sauvage	soh-vazh
win (to)	gagner	gan-yay
wind	le vent	vah^{n}
window	la fenêtre	fe^{r}-netr
wine	le vin	va^{n}
wine list	la carte des vins	kart day va^{n}
wine waiter	le sommelier	so-me^{r}-lyay
wing	l'aile *f*	lel
winter	l'hiver *m*	lee-vair

wish (to)	souhaiter	swe-tay
with	avec	avek
without	sans	sah[n]
woman	la femme	fam
wood	le bois	bwa
wool	la laine	len
word	le mot	mo
worse	pire	peer
worth (to be)	valoir	val-war
wound	la blessure	bles-u[e]r
wrap	envelopper	ah[n]-vlop-ay
wrist	le poignet	pwan-yay
write (to)	écrire	ay-kreer
writing paper	le papier à lettre	pap-yay a letr
wrong	incorrect	a[n]-kor-ekt

X

x-ray	la radio(graphie)	ra-dyo

Y

yacht	le yacht/le bateau à voile	yot/ba-toh a vwal
year	l'an *m*/l'année *f*	lah[n]/la-nay

yellow	jaune	zhohn
yes	oui	we
yesterday	hier	yair
you	vous	voo
young	jeune	zhœn
your	votre *s*/vos *pl*	votr/voh
yours	le/la vôtre	vohtr
youth hostel	l'auberge de jeunesse *f*	loh-bairzh de^{r} zhœ-nes

Z

zip	la fermeture éclair	fair-me^{r}-tu^{e}r ay-klair
zoo	le zoo	zoh

Notes

Notes

Notes

Notes

Notes

Notes

Notes